TWAYNE'S WORLD AUTHORS SERIES

A Survey of the World's Literature

Sylvia E. Bowman, Indiana University

GENERAL EDITOR

GERMANY

Ulrich Weisstein, Indiana University

EDITOR

Wolfram von Eschenbach

(*TWAS* 233)

TWAYNE'S WORLD AUTHORS SERIES (TWAS)

*The purpose of TWAS is to survey the major writers
—novelists, dramatists, historians, poets, philosophers,
and critics—of the nations of the world. Among the
national literatures covered are those of Australia,
Canada, China, Eastern Europe, France, Germany,
Greece, India, Italy, Japan, Latin America, the
Netherlands, New Zealand, Poland, Russia, Scan-
dinavia, Spain, and the African nations, as well as
Hebrew, Yiddish, and Latin Classical literatures. This
survey is complemented by Twayne's United States
Authors Series and English Authors Series.*

*The intent of each volume in these series is to present
a critical-analytical study of the works of the writer;
to include biographical and historical material that
may be necessary for understanding, appreciation,
and critical appraisal of the writer; and to present all
material in clear, concise English—but not to vitiate
the scholarly content of the work by doing so.*

Wolfram von Eschenbach

By JAMES F. POAG

Indiana University

Twayne Publishers, Inc. :: New York

MANUFACTURED IN THE UNITED STATES OF AMERICA

1-29-85

1730482

To my parents

Preface

In keeping with the aims of this series, I have endeavored to present a critical-analytical study of the works of Wolfram von Eschenbach, along with a discussion of relevant aspects of the author's life and times. Although I have undertaken to discuss important points of scholarly controversy in the text, I have, at the same time, relegated many of the details on such matters to the footnotes. I believe that this is also in keeping with the aims of the series.

Middle High German quotations from Wolfram's works are taken from the sixth Lachmann edition, quotations from Gott-fried von Strassburg's *Tristan* from the edition prepared by Werner Schröder (Berlin: De Gruyter, 1969). The citation from Walther von der Vogelweide is taken from the *Studienausgabe* prepared by Hugo Kuhn (Berlin: De Gruyter, 1965). Portions of the short subchapter on "Gahmuret and Gawan" are taken from my unpublished dissertation completed, in 1961, at the University of Illinois.

I am especially indebted to the book on Wolfram von Eschen-bach written by Joachim Bumke for the Metzlar Verlag series, as well as to Bumke's books on *Willehalm* and on Wolfram scholar-ship since 1945 (cf. Selected Bibliography, pp. 130 ff. under B, C, & H). I have tried to acknowledge my considerable debt to other scholars in the notes that accompany this volume. I would also like to express my gratitude to the following institutions and persons:

To Indiana University, to the Fulbright Commission, and to the Alexander von Humboldt Foundation for grants to do research on Wolfram von Eschenbach.

To Walter de Gruyter & Co., Berlin, for permission to quote from those editions of the works of Wolfram von Eschenbach, Gottfried von Strassburg, and Walther von der Vogelweide men-tioned above.

To Random House for permission to quote from the Helen Mustard and Charles E. Passage translation of *Parzival* (the English equivalents given in this volume for *Parzival* are taken from that version).

To Penguin Books for permission to quote from A. T. Hatto's translation of *Tristan* (the English equivalents given for *Tristan* in this volume are taken from there).

To Professor Ulrich Weisstein for his excellent editorial advice.

To my wife Juliane for her help and encouragement.

JAMES F. POAG

Indiana University, Bloomington

Contents

Chronology

CHAPTER 1

History and Biography

I *The Historical Moment*

WOLFRAM von Eschenbach was born during the reign of Emperor Frederic Barbarossa. The chronicles describe this German emperor most favorably. With his great stature, his excellent constitution, his energy, his pleasant manner, his valor, and his sense of moderation he seemed to those who knew him a personification of the newly constituted chivalric ideals.[1]

Frederic was an astute politician.[2] He was able to maintain a modicum of unity and tranquility in fragmented, feudal Germany. It was no simple task, arbitrating barons' quarrels, resisting their encroachments on his own power, maintaining a truce between the rival houses of the Guelfs and the Hohenstaufen, countering the influence of the Pope in Germany's affairs. Frederic gave the Empire new economic life. He encouraged shipping on the Rhine and industry in the cities, reasserted the imperial claims to the revenues of Northern Italy, and betrothed his son Henry to Constance of Sicily, one of the wealthiest heiresses in Europe. He secured the gold necessary for maintaining a dependable army and efficient administration. He built and garrisoned a vast network of castles and keeps ruled from a core in Swabia, Alsace, the Palatinate, and Franconia. Frederic relied on the service of ministerials, soldiers and administrators without land of their own, and upon bishops of the German church. Both groups were directly responsible to him and served as a political and military counterweight in his struggle with the relatively independent and unreliable German lords.

Italy figured strongly in Barbarossa's political calculations; and France too played an important role in his strategy. On the feast of Pentecost in 1156, he married Beatrice of Burgundy and began to administer large portions of southern France in her name. The Chronicles record numerous imperial trips to this region during the following years (Count Rupert of Durne, one of Wolfram von Eschenbach's patrons, is listed among Frederic's companions on such journeys). Only a decade before Frederic's marriage to Beatrice, 140,000 warriors from France and Germany had undertaken a Crusade to the Holy Land. The Crusade had been preached in Germany by the French mystic Bernard of Clairvaux, who had spoken in the major German churches and had won the old Emperor Conrad over to the war. Now, under Frederic Barbarossa, the contacts between French and Germans grew considerably, particularly on the Rhine. The ultimate symbolic expression of Barbarossa's success was the great courtly festival at Pentecost in 1184. In that year, the European nobility gathered in Mayence to witness the knighting of Barbarossa's sons. Huge tents, halls, and enclosures were erected for the pageantry, the feasting, the tournaments, and the games. Flagged ships floated on the Rhine and great quantities of excellent food and drink were consumed. Poets and chroniclers were to refer to the immensely costly event for a long time afterwards.

In 1187 the army of the Mohammedan leader Saladin captured Jerusalem. Saladin's spirit of generosity impressed his Christian enemies, but they were determined to recapture the Holy City. In the spring of the following year, Frederic Barbarossa vowed to undertake a Crusade; two years later, the Emperor was dead, drowned by the weight of his own armor in a river in the Orient. It was a turn of events from which the institution of the Empire was never to recover.

Henry, Barbarossa's son, attempted to take charge and execute his father's policies, but he became entangled in Italian ventures. He was forced to move quickly against a party of Sicilian nationalists, who had plotted his assassination in an attempt to free the island of German rule. Henry was adroit and clever, but also ruthless and cruel. He had managed to imprison Richard the Lion-Hearted in his Palatinate castle of Trifels, and he had eventually collected an exorbitant ransom for him. With money in hand and Saladin dead (1193), Henry planned to carry out the Crusade which his father had left unfinished, avoiding the land route to Palestine that had proven so disastrous to German armies in the past. He had already gathered a fleet and sent an army east when, in 1197, at the age of thirty-three, he caught the plague. He died in Palermo, leaving a son, Frederic Roger, who was three years old.

Henry's brother, Philip, who had been destined for the priesthood, now was forced to become the ruler of Germany, at a time when Innocent III had ascended the papal throne, fully intent on bringing the old unsettled quarrel between the Empire and the Papacy to an end. The new Pope supported Otto the Guelf, who seemed amenable to the Church, as his candidate for emperor, and managed to have him crowned. Philip, who had been elected emperor by the German princes, had a gentle and trusting nature. He was repeatedly betrayed, notably by Hermann, the powerful prince of Thuringia, but he was nevertheless able in the course of time to consolidate his position. Victory seemed almost within reach when, in 1208, he was murdered. Otto was now master of the Empire and quickly became the natural enemy of his old ally, Innocent. Innocent countered by turning to Henry Hohenstaufen's son, Frederic Roger, who had come of age. The Pope was determined to use this young man as a pawn in his struggle with the Empire. Frederic eventually won the crown, with the Pope's help, only to turn against him, just as Otto had done before him. To many observers it seemed that the age of the Anti-Christ had come. A protracted war between Imperial and Papal forces decimated the Empire, tainted the Papacy, and encouraged factionalism and cynicism. The Germans had seen a promise in Barbarossa's reign, but they had been disappointed. The Minnesinger Walther von der Vogelweide, appalled by this spectacle of slow dissolution, wrote a number of trenchant anti-papal poems. Toward the end of his life, the old master poet, a contemporary and acquaintance of Wolfram von Eschenbach, composed an elegy lamenting the death of those courtly ways which Barbarossa had seemed to personify. Toward the end of his life, Walther turned his thought to a Crusade, but that venture too had become suspect, for the Christian Crusaders' greedy and vicious sack of Constantinople in 1204 had generated a lasting shock. But let us turn to a discussion of knightly culture.

A recent study of the German word for "knight" [3] shows that this term (*riter, ritter*) was more loosely applied than we would, perhaps, expect. It could, for example, be used to describe the simple foot soldier as well as the heavily mailed warrior on horseback,

and the serving man of the palace as well as the mercenary man
of arms. In most cases, the person so designated was a member of
some retinue or household. It seems likely, therefore, that the
word was used to characterize service relationships. *Ritter* were
simply men in the pay of a lord. This explains why the term could
not, initially, be applied to kings.

The concept's semantic range was significantly widened during
the last decades of the twelfth century. Under Barbarossa and his
sons, the French notion of chivalry grew popular. The Arthurian
romances of Chrestien de Troyes were reworked in German and
popularized the ethos of the French *chevalier.* The associations
which had accrued to the French term were almost immediately
transferred to the German word *ritter,* and the colorless label now
became the focal point in a growing literary movement. In the
years between 1180 and 1200, Hartmann von Aue, a ministerial
from Swabia, translated Chrestien's *Erec* and his *Iwein* in a pol-
ished manner. The German *Iwein,* with its "light" style, was in
fact considered the perfect literary expression of that chief
knightly virtue, moderation, and the motifs of this Arthurian romance (with enchanted lands, surly giants, and maidens in distress) offered ample opportunity for reflection upon the nature of
adventure and courtly love, the two major concerns of chivalric
literature.[4]

As Kalogreant, the questing Arthurian knight, tries to explain to
a hairy denizen of the forest (*Iwein,* 528 ff.), adventure is the
active, persistent search for combat; it entails a life of discomfort
and struggle cultivated for its own sake. Here the ethos of service
has been freed from thought of material reward and *ritters ambet*
(the office of knight) has been sublimated. Iwein's adventures are
not only proof of his prowess and the source of worldly honor.
They are, above all, a commitment to help the needy and the
weak with lance and sword. They are the knight's way to spiritual
perfection.

This knightly ideal of sublimated service found nourishment in
the cult of love.[5] The courtly poet sang of how he longed to see
his lady-liege, how he hoped for a glance or a discreet nod from
her as a reward for continued faithfulness. His beloved was, however, characteristically married to another. Moreover, the poet's
enemies, villainous spies, were often an impediment to the physi-

cal consummation of love. The courtly writer, like his clerical counterpart, the twelfth-century mystic, found himself immersed in contemplation. Reinmar von Hagenau, for example, the German master of *Minnesang*, loved to analyze his heart and observe how his emotions shifted from a state of doubt to a mood of exhilaration and back again to doubt. Reinmar carefully nurtured each sign that the lady did return his feelings. If his beloved did seem unresponsive, callous, and cruel, he mused, it was because she had to feign indifference. She wished to test his capacity for endurance and his strength of spirit. In her goodness she wanted to lift him morally and to show him the joy of continued renunciation. Reinmar prided himself, above all, on his ability to suffer with tempered grace.

Such lyric poetry thrives on romantic paradox. The poet, through a leap of faith, reaffirms the substance of love where only shadows seem to lie. In all this he comes to discover his "higher self." Happy merely in the triumph of his will, he awaits the distant day of his lady's grace. Courtly poetry is, of course, a social phenomenon, a game, a playful cult. It appears, at the same time, to be a serious attempt to secularize religious teaching; and the medieval mystic's experience of the soul's search for the grace of God is quite analogous to the medieval poet's ceaseless importuning of his lady, whose mind, it seems, he can scarcely come to know. The chivalric lyric is thus a curious mixture of entertainment and spiritual exaltation; it offers perspectives that reach from eroticism to the ascetic sublimation of passion, from earnest idealism to parody of love's own tenets.

The new literature, which idealized women, was propagated and popularized in Europe by a woman, Eleanor of Aquitaine,[6] who had had two unhappy marriages. The spirit of courtly love must have spoken to such women, whose husbands were chosen for them on the basis of political consideration. The new literature opposed such a state of affairs. True love must be a free gift, the theory of courtly love argued; love cannot exist in marriage, which legislates personal surrender. True love, therefore, must find fulfillment *outside* the marriage bond. Here was a curious situation: Christians using the arguments of Christian philosophy in order to undermine Christian morality. Subtle mockery of religion or transposition of its tenets were, in fact, assiduously cultivated by some, and it is symptomatic that the two great romances of "adultery," *Tristan* and *Lancelot,* should have been written at this time.

Clearly, the outlook of the general public in Europe had reached a turning point. Even in Germany the perspective of vernacular poetry reveals the existence of a lay audience increasingly interested in a wide range of intellectual and artistic questions. This is something new.[7] As a consequence of the barbarian invasions and the collapse of Roman civilization, from the sixth century on there had been no general audience in the West capable of sustaining a "sophisticated" literary culture. Reading and writing had become the province of the monasteries, and secular leaders had had little to do with learning. Literature had been purveyed, in part, by public entertainers, and, in part, by churchmen, who had an interest in extending their influence through this medium. In the early Middle Ages, such churchmen carried out their mission by composing religious poetry for the laity—in the vernacular. During the twelfth century, however, they began to devote themselves with greater frequency to secular themes. Latin literature too became increasingly accessible during these years. The schools and universities started to produce larger numbers of lay "clerks" versed in the Latin tongue. Goliard poets began to compose Latin love and drinking songs, and to revel in satire and parody of the Church, its teachings and its sacraments. (One of the most famous and talented of their number, the Archpoet, belonged to the household of Rainald von Dassel, Barbarossa's chancellor.) Men with ecclesiastical education, but without holy orders, came to have an increasing influence on the cultural life at European courts. Tightly organized scribal centers made book production cheaper. Princes and patrons could more easily acquire the manuscript sources which their poets needed. There was a growing interpenetration, a cross-fertilization between the world of learning and the world of lay literary activity. Lay poets now began to produce a really significant vernacular literature. This literature was opened to the influence of the rhetorical style, which had been cultivated in the Latin literature of the Middle Ages, it was fashioned into a vehicle capable of expressing the subtleties and nuances of the human psyche (something that had been possible hitherto only in the Latin writings of the mystics).

Wolfram von Eschenbach lived and wrote in this "age of re-awakening." He reflected on the nature of human society, the source of disorder in governmental systems, and the tragedy of the Crusades. He examined the new style, chivalric culture, and courtly love. He tested the relationship of man to woman and that of men to God. The conclusions at which he arrived are still significant.

II *Wolfram's Personal Background*

We have no record of the precise date of Wolfram von Eschenbach's birth; but on the basis of the poet's references to contemporary events we can reconstruct and fix it at about 1170. Although we cannot identify Wolfram's place of birth with absolute certainty, the evidence speaks convincingly for the small Franconian town of Ober-Eschenbach which is located a few miles southwest of Nuremberg.[8] Wolfram's dialect points to this area, and the little village itself lies near several obscure places to which Wolfram refers, with a knowledge of local details. He speaks of sizzling fritters, the specialty of "Trühendingen" (Wassertrüdingen), a town southwest of Ober-Eschenbach (*P.* 184, 24–25). He knows the condition of a jousting field in "Abenberc," east of Ober-Eschenbach (*P.* 227, 9–13), and comments on the shrovetide customs of the market wives in "Tolenstein" (Dollenstein), southeast of that town (*P.* 409, 5–11). He is also acquainted with "der Sant," a stretch of land east of Ober-Eschenbach (*Wh.* 426, 28–30).[9]

There are still other "proofs." In *Parzival,* Wolfram addresses (*P.* 184, 4) a certain Count of Wertheim. Although Wertheim is located on the Main quite a distance from Ober-Eschenbach, it is known that the Counts of Wertheim had holdings in the Franconian village. Wolfram could well have been their vassal. In the *Eichstätt Book of Fiefs* (which documents the feudal structure of the area in question) there is an undated reference to a family of petty noblemen which designates certain children of this family as *pueri Wolframi de Eschenbach.*[10]

Finally, we have the testimony of two observers who tell us, several centuries later, that they saw the grave of the poet in Our Lady's Minster in Ober-Eschenbach. Jakob Püterich von Reichertshausen writes in 1462 that Wolfram was, indeed, buried in this church and that the grave had an epitaph with Wolfram's coat of arms, but that the exact date of his death could not be deci-

phered.[11] A Nuremberg patrician, H. W. Kress, confirms this testimony in 1608 and records an inscription which he saw upon
the grave: "Here lies the Doughty Knight Sir Wolfram von
Eschenbach, a Master Singer." The style of the original German
inscription betrays its time of composition (the term Master
Singer, for example, was coined in the later Middle Ages). But if
it is true that the inscription and probably the coat of arms were
the product of the fourteenth century, the grave itself should be
regarded as authentic.

The question of Wolfram's birth leads us to that of his social
status. Poets like Wirnt von Gravenberg (in *Wigalois*, 1. 6346)
and Ulrich von Eschenbach (in *Alexander*, 1. 127) praise Wolfram's work with the formula: "Layman's mouth ne'er spoke better." The designation can be accepted. Although intensely
interested in religious questions, Wolfram sets the accents in such
a way that it is clear that he really was a layman—writing for
laymen. But if there is no doubt about this and the fact that he
was linked with men like the Count of Wertheim, it is more difficult to ascertain his exact place in the social hierarchy. Was he
really a member of the petty nobility, as we surmise? It is true
that Wolfram says of himself: "schildes ambet ist mîn art" (*P.*
115, 11),* but this statement is ambiguous for, even if Wolfram
was a nobleman, his social position could not have been impres-
sive.[12] He must have been poor, possibly a younger son, and therefore ineligible for inheritance (cf. *P.* 4, 27–5, 10). Only one thing
is certain: as a man and poet he was totally committed to probing
the implications of the chivalric way of life. In *Parzival* and *Willehalm* he transformed the knightly calling into a poetic symbol of
man struggling toward spirituality.

A close reading of Wolfram's works would seem to tell us that
he was a devoted father and husband. Wolfram's preoccupation
with his own family may well have generated basic poetic themes
and symbols, as did his fascination with the implications of the
knightly calling. From remarks made in *Parzival* and *Willehalm*
we gain the impression that Wolfram had a daughter who was
very dear to him (*P.* 367, 21–29; *Wh.* 33, 24–26). He believed
children to be one of the greatest joys that could come to man:
"mit rehter kiusche erworben kint,/ich waene diu smannes saelde

* "My birth was to the knightly trade."

sint" (*P.* 743, 21–22).* Did the poet project the apparent tenderness he had for his own daughter into his disarming portrayals of
the many children to be found in his oeuvre: young Parzivâl and
Rennewart, little Obilôt, Sigûne, and Schîânatulander? At one
point Wolfram refers with humorous affection to his wife (*P.* 216,
28 ff). Did his love for her have an influence on him while writing
Parzival and *Willehalm?* In these poems, the German anthor developed the theme of a man's longing for his distant wife into a
major spiritual problem. Wolfram's calculated transformation of
the traditional content of the dawn song (from adulterous to conjugal love) may certainly be considered typical of his tendency to
emphasize the sacredness of marriage.[13]

III *Wolfram's Patrons and His Public*

While describing the siege of Pelrapeire, Wolfram refers to a
certain Count of Wertheim (*P.* 183, 24 ff). He points out that this
Count, his master, would hardly have liked to have been a soldier
in that city, where famine reigned, where the citizens had neither
cheese nor meat nor bread, where no man had need for tooth-
picks, and where neither fat dripped nor pancakes popped nor
tankards brimmed. We know something of the Wertheims, a
proud and influential family.[14] Some *Parzival* manuscripts actually
identify Wolfram's Count, calling him Poppe (or Boppe). This is
in agreement with historical records. There are, in fact, two
Counts of Wertheim who must be considered, Poppo I
(1165–1212) and his son Poppo II (1212–1238). The dates of the
father would best suit our chronology of Wolfram, and his inclina-
tions Wolfram's allusion. Poppo I was a man who would not have
liked to live in famine, as the following self-characterization indicates: "Ego Boppo dei gratia Comes de Wertheym nobilitate
praepollens, diviciis deliciisque affluens."

In 1189 Poppo, like so many so many of his peers, joined the
Crusade of Frederic Barbarossa. The ideology of this undertaking
must have been important to the court, and it was perhaps in this
connection that Wolfram extended the epic horizon of his source
for *Parzival* beyond the fairy-tale world of Arthurian adventure
and into the world of the Orient, shaping a myth of Christian rule

* "Children chastely born, I ween, / Have many a man's salvation
been."

over the heathen territories. But Poppo was not the only one of Wolfram's benefactors to take the cross, and the work of Wolfram's old age, *Willehalm,* probes deeper into the problem of the Crusade by exploring the tragedy of a war of slaughter waged in the name of God.

In our efforts to reconstruct the pertinent aspects of Wolfram's public life, we are helped by a remark which the poet makes in Book V of *Parzival.* Referring to the luxurious size of the fireplaces in the Grail Castle, the poet compares these to the fireplace at the castle of Wildenberg. He says: "sô grôziu fiwer sît noch ê/sach niemen *hie* ze Wildenberc" (230, 12–13).* Wolfram must have been in a castle named Wildenberg at the time he made his statement. It is possible that he was then, in fact, living in a *burc* (Wildenburg) whose walls still dominate a hill in the Odenwald near Amorbach, south of the Main and not far from Wertheim. Sir Rupert von Durne (1171–1197) probably was the lord of this castle at the time when Wolfram made his remark. Like Count Poppo, he was an important figure in imperial society. His castle is now a ruin, razed in the Peasants' War, but it still shows signs of its former splendor. In the great hall, where in Wolfram's time poets may have gathered to recite before the assembled knights and ladies, there is a huge ornamented fireplace. Is Wolfram laughing at Rupert, a devoted builder, when he states that those fireplaces in the Grail Castle were larger than Rupert's great stone fireplace? Carved into the southeast wall of this castle are the words *owe• mvter,* an obvious reference to one of the most famous lines in Wolfram's works, Parzivâl's question to his mother: "ôwê muoter, waz ist got?" (*P.* 119, 17), that is: "O, what is God, Mother?" The name which Wolfram gives to the Grail Castle, *Munsalvaesche,* might even be a translation of *Wildenberg: munt salvage* (*mont sauvage*), *mons silvaticus.*[15] Perhaps Wolfram was attempting to honor this lord, who was his patron, when he inserted the designation.[16] Rupert's circle of acquaintances was wide. He had extensive connections with the German nobility (among these the Counts of Wertheim) as well as contacts with Frenchmen like Count Philip of Flanders. Philip had provided the French *romancier* Chrestien de Troyes with the source (*le livre*) for his *Perceval,* and Chrestien's *Perceval* was—in turn—to be the major source for

---

* "Such great fires no one has ever seen *here* in Wildenberg before or since." [Italics are mine].

Wolfram's *Parzival*. It is possible that Wolfram's decision to write his first epic work goes back ultimately to a personal exchange between the two literary enthusiasts, Philip and Rupert, and that—as result of their personal contact—Chrestien's story of the Grail made its way from France to Germany and Wolfram. But this is pure speculation.

We can only guess at the manner in which Wolfram came upon the French source for his *Parzival*, but we know with certainty who it was that alerted him to the French source for his later work *Willehalm*. Wolfram himself tells us: "lantgrâf von Dürngen Herman/tet mir diz maer . . . bekant" (*Wh.* 3, 8–9).* Hermann, Landgrave of Thuringia from 1190 until 1217, lord of the Neuenburg, the Grimmenstein and the Wartburg, was a man rich and powerful enough to challenge the authority of the German Emperors. Quick to act for his own advantage, he was not hampered by scrupulous loyalties, and in the struggle for the imperial throne in Germany, which took place during Wolfram's lifetime, he effortlessly and repeatedly changed sides. Now for, then against Henry VI, Philip of Swabia, Otto IV, and Frederic II, he came to be known as Hermann the Faithless. He was the father-in-law of Saint Elisabeth of Hungary who came to Thuringia as a child to be betrothed to his son Ludwig. Hermann took part in Barbarossa's Crusade of 1189. In his youth he had been in France, and here he had taken a liking to French literature. When his older brother (also a participant in the Third Crusade) died on Cyprus, he became "Landgrave" of Thuringia.

Legend tells us of the *Wartburgkrieg*, the famous contest of the great singers which allegedly took place at Hermann's court in 1206 and 1207, that is, at a time when Wolfram must have been at the height of his poetic powers. The participants in this clash were, according to the legend, Heinrich von Ofterdingen, Walther von der Vogelweide, Wolfram von Eschenbach, Reinmar von Zweter, Heinrich der Schreiber, and Biterolf. In the *Wartburgkrieg* legend, Wolfram, though a layman, possesses unsurpassed wisdom and is more than a match for the infernal arts of his adversary, the sorcerer Klingsor. Some sort of truth must lie at the heart of this tale, for Hermann of Thuringia was actually the patron of a number of German poets, among them Heinrich von

* "Landgrave Hermann of Thuringia made known this tale . . . to me."

Veldeke, Herbort von Fritzlar, and Walther von der Vogelweide.
Wolfram, too, received support from him.

Life at Hermann's court was, it seems, loud and chaotic, and
not in keeping with the chivalric rules of propriety. Hermann's
generosity evidently attracted all sorts of people to his service. In
Wolfram's day, it was the custom among courtly writers to con-
demn the harsh manners of King Arthur's seneschal Keye, but
Wolfram does the opposite. He praises Keye in order to draw
attention to the lack of discipline at Hermann's court:

> . . .
> er [Keye] tet vil rûhes willen schîn
> ze scherme dem hêrren sîn:
> partierre und valsche diet,
> von den werden er die schiet:
> er was ir vuore ein strenger hagel,
> noch scherpfer dan der bîn ir zagel.   (P. 297, 7–12) *

Addressing Hermann directly, Wolfram says:

> von Dürgen fürste Herman,
> etslîch dîn ingesinde ich maz,
> daz ûzgesinde hieze baz.
> dir waere och eines Keien nôt,
> sît wâriu milte dir gebôt
> sô manecvalten anehanc,
> etswâ smaehlîch gedranc
> unt etswâ werdez dringen.
> des muoz hêr Walther singen
> 'guoten tac, boes unde guot.'   (P. 297, 16–25) †

Although the song of Walther von der Vogelweide to which Wolfram refers has not been preserved, we do have a similar poem

* ". . . the harshness which he [Keye] displayed was for the protec-
tion of his lord. Tricksters and hypocrites he separated from the noble
folk, and on them he descended like harsh hail, sharper than the sting
of a bee's tail.

† "Herman, Prince of Thuringia, some of those I have seen residing *in*
your house should better be residing *out*. You too could use a Keie, for
your true generosity has brought you a motley following, in part a
mean and worthless band, in part a noble throng. This is why Sir
Walther sings, 'I greet you one and all, the base and the good.' "

written by Walther. It supports in every way the negative picture
Wolfram draws of Hermann's court:

> Der in den ôren siech von ungesühte sî,
> daz ist mîn rât, der lâz den hof ze Dürengen frî:
> wan kumet er dar, dêswâr er wirt ertoeret.
> ich hân gedrungen unz ich niht mê dringen mac.
> ein schar vert ûz, diu ander in, naht unde tac.
> grôz wunder ist daz iemen dâ gehoeret.
> der lantgrâve ist sô gemuot
> daz er mit stolzen helden sîne habe vertuot,
> der iegeslîcher wol ein kenpfe waere.   (*WvV*, 20, 4)*

There has been speculation about Wolfram's personal life at
court. Did he actually have an "affair" with one of the ladies in
Hermann's entourage and, if so, was it a real affair of the heart or
just a literary game, love, or flattering attention paid by a needy
poet to a woman of rank? Wolfram speaks of his "violent passion"
in Book VI of *Parzival* (*P*. 287, 10 ff.). He indicates that the romance was written to gain the favor of a woman (*P*. 337, 27–30;
827, 29–30). In Book VIII of *Parzival* he interrupts his tale to
digress on the virtues of a certain Countess of Heitstein (*P*. 403,
29–404, 6). He seems to praise this lady, and we know that there
was such a person, that she was widowed and still young in 1204,
and that her sister Sophia was the second wife of Hermann of
Thuringia. Did Wolfram meet the widow at Hermann's court and
fall in love with her? And was she the woman for whom he wrote
his *Parzival*? In comparing the Countess to Antikonîe, the heroine
of one of Gâwân's erotic adventures, Wolfram was in fact doing
her no favor. Actually Wolfram's apparent praise of her is filled
with impertinent sexual allusions. Considering her rank, Wolfram's
poetic license must have been great, although he evidently did not
escape entirely unscathed either. His insult of the Countess seems
to have earned him the enmity of other ladies at the court (*P*. 114,
5 ff.; 337, 1 ff.).

* "Whoever has sensitive ears, I advise him, don't go near the court of
Thuringia. For whoever comes there, I swear, he'll go mad. I've joined
that din, until I can no longer bear it. One troops leaves, another
arrives—day and night. It's a miracle that anyone still has ears to hear
there. The Landgrave is of such a mind that he throws away his wealth
on high-spirited fighters."

All these allusions provoke our interest. We cannot fit the pieces together as we would like to do but we do gain from the scattered bits a heightened appreciation of Wolfram's provocative attitude toward his public and something of an impression of the life that prevailed at the courts of the men he served: Poppo, for example, who lived joyously and well, but who was moved to undertake the penance of a Crusade; Hermann, with his scandalous, raucous entourage, but with a saint for a daughter-in-law. These lords and the people around them must have been singularly receptive to Wolfram's peculiar style, to his blend of high spirituality and good-humored rudeness.

CHAPTER 2

Wolfram's Literary Outlook

THE "better" poets of the high Middle Ages were concerned with questions of formal technique. It was considered important to know the prosodic rules, to master the art of rhyming, and to control the level of one's style. There was prestige in book learning. A poet who could boast of his knowledge of tongues, rhetoric, law, music, and other fields was held in high esteem. It is generally believed, however, that Wolfram von Eschenbach had formal training in few if any of these disciplines. He was a man of simple family, a soldier and not a "clerk." He wrote in a style that was—comparatively speaking—rough-hewn, and his knowledge, though broad, appears to have been unsystematic.[1] Most scholars believe that he understood little Latin.[2] His French, many think, was faulty also, picked up possibly as he accompanied his patrons on trips to France. Wolfram himself tells us that he *spoke* French badly,[3] and it has in fact been held that he could not *read* at all. The poet's own words seem to bear this out:

> ine kan decheinen buochstap.
> dâ nement genuoge ir urhap:
> disiu âventiure
> vert âne der buoche stiure   (P. 115, 27–30)*

Internal evidence appears to support the thesis that Wolfram was unlettered, and that he was forced to acquire his literary material aurally.[4] We know that he experienced difficulty with his French sources,[5] that he tended to confuse initial French sounds, and to reverse the line sequence of the French original (mistakes commonly made when material is dictated). Wolfram's style,

---

* "*I don't know a single letter of the alphabet.* Plenty of people get their material that way, *but this adventure steers without books.*" [Italics mine].

moreover, is characterized by considerable syntactical and metrical liberty, and this would seem to point to the practice of oral composition. Finally, although he repeatedly refers to his sources, Wolfram never informs us that he *read* anything in them. It is always "my tale *said*," "I *heard* tell."

It is possible that, as an illiterate, Wolfram had a reader and scribe assigned to him. This would help explain his ability to arrange a tale of such length. We must exercise some caution, however. All the evidence cited thus far cannot be regarded as absolutely conclusive. Wolfram's own statement on the matter of *buoche* and *buochstap* should not be taken at face value and has to be further examined. Wolfram, who loved to ornament his work with grotesque motifs, seems to have been involved in a feud with educated poets who were not amused by the Franconian's bizarre tastes. One of these poets, Gottfried von Strassburg, seems to have criticized Wolfram for his treatment of the *Parzival* material. Wolfram had apparently bastardized his French source; he had, if we understand Gottfried correctly, accomplished this by using elements from "base" literary traditions. Gottfried writes concerning Wolfram:

> *vindaere wilder maere,*
> *der maere wildenaere,*
> die mit den ketenen liegent
> und stumpfe sinne triegent
> die golt von *swachen sachen*
> den kinden kunnen machen
> und uz der bühsen giezen
> *stoubine mergriezen:*   (*T.* 4663–4670) *

Perhaps Wolfram's statement on *buoche* and *buochstap* was in fact a rebuttal intended for Gottfried. If so, Wolfram could have been using the word *buoche*—as French poets did the word *livre* —to designate his "written source";[6] he may at the same time have had in mind an additional nuance, the use of *buoche* as *terminus technicus* for the Latin *auctores*,[7] those classical writers

---

* "*Inventors of wild tales, hired hunters after stories,* who cheat with chains and dupe dull minds, who turn *rubbish* into gold for children and from magic boxes pour *pearls of dust!*" The word *vindaere* of course need not be translated as "inventor." The Middle High German could simply mean "*writers*" of wild tales.

whom Gottfried and his kind admired for their purity in matters of taste and style. Moreover, the passage containing Wolfram's polemic comment on the uselessness of "books" is almost surely an interpolation. Wolfram could have inserted it after having been provoked by Gottfried's critique. In any case, if we do project Wolfram's statement on "books" into a framework of literary feud, and if we do invest his term (*buoche*) with this technical meaning, an interesting interpretation emerges. Wolfram would be defending his right to poetic fantasy, however bizarre and supposedly crude. He would be declaring himself absolutely unconcerned with that devotion to "taste" which Gottfried seems to demand of him. In effect, he would not be saying: "I am illiterate" but rather: "this adventure steers without *buoche*," without particular concern either for its source (*livre*) or the *auctores*, i.e., for that level of style which classically educated writers might hope to dictate. With this possible interpretation of the statement in mind, we must direct ourselves to further consideration of medieval literary theory.

Gottfried von Strassburg knew and approved the teachings he found in Latin books on style. Following rhetorical prescriptions he praised the "light" style characteristic of Hartmann von Aue's writing and damned the "dark" manner typical of Wolfram's poetry:[8]

> Hartman der Ouwaere
> ahi, wie der diu maere
> beide uzen unde innen
> mit worten und mit sinnen
> *durchverwet* und *durchzieret!*
> wie er mit rede *figieret*
> der aventiure meine!
> wie luter and wie reine
> sine kristallinen wortelin
> beidiu sint und iemer müezen sin!
> si koment den man mit siten an,
> si tuont sich nahe zuo dem man
> und liebent rehtem muote.
> swer guote rede ze guote
> und ouch ze rehte kan verstan,
> der muoz dem Ouwaere lan
> sin schapel und sin lorzwi.
> swer nu des hasen geselle si

und uf der wortheide
hochsprünge und witweide
mit bickelworten welle sin
und uf daz lorschapelekin
wan ane volge welle han,
der laze uns bi dem wane stan;
wir wellen an der kür ouch wesen.   (*T.* 4619–4643) *

Gottfried's commentary on Hartmann and Wolfram is again full of technical terms. The words *durchverwet* und *figieret*, for example, are a translation from the Latin and refer to the *colores et figurae rhetorici* which Hartmann used in embellishing his tale. Gottfried has, in fact, borrowed his entire exposition—on "inner" and "outer" narrative elements, on clear and transparent words, on garland, laurels, and Poetry's heath—from a body of Latin rhetorical treatise,[9] and it is obvious that Gottfried's classical laurels for style will in the end be awarded to Hartmann, not to Wolfram.

This brings us to a discussion of the shadings that might be contained in Wolfram's seemingly straightforward remark: "Ine kan decheinen buochstap" ("I don't know a single letter of the alphabet"). Medieval exegetical tradition commonly used the Latin word *litteratura* as a designation for that letter of the law which kills the spirit; since the medieval German equivalent for *litteratura* was *buochstap*,[10] Wolfram's statement might, therefore, have had this thrust: "I know nothing of *that letter of the law* (*buochstap*) which kills the spirit." That is hardly an admission of illiteracy. The theme clearly occupied Wolfram's attention. In *Willehalm* (*Wh.* 2, 19 ff.), for instance, he again declared himself independent of the *buochen* and indicated that his real inspiration came from the Holy Ghost. If we consider the passages in *Parzival*

* "Ah, how Hartmann of Aue dyes and adorns his tales through and through with words and sense, both outside and within! How eloquently he establishes his story's meaning! How clear and transparent his crystal words both are and ever must remain! Gently they approach and fawn on a man, and captivate right minds. Those who esteem fine language with due sympathy and judgment will allow the man of Aue his garland and his laurels.

But if some friend of the hare [Wolfram] high-skipping and far-browsing, seeks out Poetry's heath with dicing terms, and lacking our general assent, aspires to the laurel wreath, let him leave us to adhere to our opinion that we too must have a hand in the choosing."

and *Willehalm* to be linked, then the whole argument must be summed up as follows: "Although other poets (namely Gottfried and his kind) are deadened by the letter of the law, I, Wolfram—despite my peculiar background and tastes—am nevertheless quickened in my poetry by the spirit that brings life, i.e., the Holy Ghost."

But let us turn more directly to a consideration of Wolfram's literary standpoint. There was a whole body of literature written, as we have seen, for the instruction of the faithful. There were, for example, great rhymed chronicles which purported to offer an account of important happenings that reached from the time of creation or from the time of the fall of Lucifer and Adam up to the present time. These vernacular works presented a traditional Augustinian view of history as the movement which would gradually reveal God's plan for man's salvation. Some of these "histories" drew part of their material from popular oral traditions, from the world of sagas, anecdotes, fairy tales, and heroic songs. The related genre of the legend was—for obvious reasons—important to these poets who rhymed in German for the edification of Christians; and here, too, there was a certain interpenetration of clerical and popular literary traditions. Tales about Old Testament figures and Christian saints were rewritten after the fashion of heroic "minstrel" poems. At the same time, "minstrel" poems dealing with the adventures of worldly heroes were bent to the task of proselytizing for the faith: rough warriors, after winning a bride, a treasure, and fame, were depicted ending their days as monks, ascetics, and saints. We find important stylistic and other features common to much of this legend and adventure poetry: a lack of rhetorical ornamentation, loose syntax, the use of formulae, inattention to prosodic detail, an author stance that tended to unite poet and public, a cultivation of hyperbole, an accumulation of the grotesque and the fabulous, and a love for oriental settings.

The clergy also produced a more ambitious literature, namely works intended for an educated audience and composed with relatively high intellectual and literary standards. Such clerical literature found its secular complement in the courtly poetry written at the close of the twelfth and the beginning of the thirteenth centuries. Hartmann's *Iwein* and Gottfried's *Tristan*, for example, quite consciously freed themselves of the antiquated stylistic features characteristic of the earlier legend and adventure tales. They assumed a cool and distant stance toward their material. They rationalized the fabulous or handled it with a light and delicious irony. Wolfram von Eschenbach seems to have been aware of these different trends and traditions. It was typical for him that he should choose to give life precisely to the popular, more primitive literary forms and attitudes which Hartmann and Gottfried had banned from their romances.

Wolfram's vocabulary betrays his affection for the old-fashioned genres. He liked using words like *recke* (warrior), *helt* (hero), *wigant* (fighting man), and *ellen* (courage), although they were considered typical of the older oral tradition and were, therefore, eschewed by Hartmann and Gottfried.[11] Even Wolfram's French has a certain primitive quality. His love of foreign terms, which he inserts in snatches, is almost excessive and contrasts oddly with his archaic vocabulary. Perhaps the unintentional (as well as intentional?) mistakes Wolfram makes in his use of the French language are the mark of a man playing the role of cultural upstart, a man who feels he is not quite acceptable but who is, in his way, proud of his crudeness and elects to play a game with other people's aspirations towards refinement. There is, of course, a significant difference between the French vocabulary of Wolfram and that of Gottfried. The French words which Wolfram included in order to stylize his work he more or less confined, quite characteristically, to areas of weaponry and knightly endeavor. Gottfried tended to avoid such terminology; but he was, on the other hand, clearly familiar with French technical terminology in esthetic and cultural matters like musical form, something which seems to have interested Wolfram little.[12]

Wolfram's vocabulary betrays a certain background, I think, namely the education and tastes of rural knightly society. Much the same could be said of his imagery.[13] The entire cosmos, the workings of men and God, are conceived of in the metaphor of the knightly calling. The battle between the devil and God for the human soul, the force of human passion, human love, and human suffering are reflected in the metaphor of the sword, lance, and trampling horse. Certain aspects of Wolfram's imagery seem to have been taken from everyday life, his own as well as that of his fellows and patrons. We find images like that of the cow whisking at flies, or the spavined horse, images of the barnyard, often barely comprehensible, but just as often capturing, in a striking figure, some homely truth. The plow, a sneezing herb, dice, a sling, a plant, the unicorn, sun and day, blossom and seed, the turtledove, a withered branch, mirth fording a flood of sorrow—these are typical of the metaphors which Wolfram used to describe human love—some transparent, others oblique and complicated, some obscene, and others exquisite. The whole wealth of a variety of "stylistic levels" is there, enlarged through an irrepressible fantasy, fed with keen powers of observation and seasoned by a sense for the absurd and grotesque.

Wolfram's syntax and style are rooted in the "primitive" genres.[14] He shouts *avoy* ("look there") and utters battle cries and interjections. His questions, illogical syntax, faulty rhymes, sudden relapses from indirect into direct speech, inversions, pleonastic and elliptical constructions, all seem to be the expression of the immediacy of his work and its conception, of his impatience to get on with the tale and to bring it closer to his listeners. There is relatively little of the carefully conceived periodic sentence structure and the practices of classical rhetoric which characterize Hartmann's and Gottfried's poetry. Hyperbole, litotes, postposited adjectives, the "poetic" word order, paratactic sentence structure, repeated recapitulation, addition of endings to foreign names, the placement of a proper name in the genitive between an article and its noun, the lack of conjunctions, the use of formulae, and even the intimate bond joining Wolfram and his public are characteristic of popular traditions.[15]

The medieval romance and epic must certainly be understood in their social context. They were festive genres, a poetry composed to be read aloud to an assembled group of people. Wolfram von Eschenbach exploited the latent possibilities of this specific situation to a greater extent than any of the contemporary German poets. His cries—"ich, Wolfram von Eschenbach!"—his advertisement of his abilities, his angry attacks, his quarrel with the ladies of the court, and his repeated references to members of the audience, all these are the product of his background and temperament and indelibly stamp his style.

Equally characteristic is Wolfram's identification of himself with the fate of his hero—now hoping, now despairing, now joyful, and now in anguish.[16] The beginning of Book IX of *Parzival* shows how effectively such a technique can be used. At this point, the audience has not glimpsed Parzivâl closely since his abrupt and ignominious departure from Plimizoel in Book VI. The hero's fate is uncertain. There are many unanswered questions as to the nature of the Grail, the Grail Castle, and everyone and everything in it. Wolfram carries on a dramatic dialogue with Lady Adventure, asking her question after question. But the answers are repeatedly postponed. We feel a tension rising in the audience. There are, perhaps, shouts and bursts of laughter as the public sees the poet playing his game with their curiosity, revealing just what he will and when he will. Wolfram flouted, of course, the standards of poets like Gottfried von Strassburg, their cultivated ideal of "well-laved" diction and "crystal" words, although he shared much of the ideal ethical and religious vocabulary of courtly culture with them. Wolfram had an exalted poetic vision, but he reveled, at the same time, in a rural sort of humor in the vital areas of food and sex.[17] In fact, the value and richness of his poetry may be seen to lie precisely in the constantly changing stance and in the clash of "styles."

Wolfram's *Parzival* and *Willehalm* were written in the form that was most common for narrative German poetry in the Middle Ages, i.e., in rhymed couplets.[18] Basic to the lines were four accented syllables, one for each of the expected four "feet." This simple scheme (which was followed with a regularity sufficient for indicating the operation of a "meter") allowed many freedoms. Before the first accented syllable, an "upbeat" of one to two, or even three, syllables was optional. Although the "foot" or "measure" was usually composed of two syllables (accented and unaccented), it could also be filled with a single accented syllable or even with one accented syllable plus two or more unaccented ones. Wolfram took particular advantage of this liberal scheme, which permitted him to adapt his line to normal rhythms of speech. Like other medieval German poets, he would fill an entire line with a single name. He would emphasize, through the use of monosyllabic measures, some important concept, a significant verb or adverb; he would call attention through this trick of prosody to important events on the surface of the narrative or the phenomena contributing to the ultimate meaning of the work. Wolfram exploited the possibilities of the metrical pattern within which he was working, varying line length, cutting or creating rhythmical and semantic connections between the end of one line and the beginning of the next, using enjambement to produce rhythmical tensions in situations in which he wished to suspend the disclosure of meaning, deliberately unsettling the metrical line, in order to create humorous effects. Critics have called Wolfram a careless poet, and some of his metrical practices, like the stylistic liberties he took, do indeed contrast with the relative prosodic clarity of his learned colleagues.[19]

Wolfram really did acquire his literary identity by cultivating the archaic and uncourtly. But at the same time he absorbed what he wished of "modern" trends. We must, therefore, examine in greater detail the nature of his attitude towards courtly style, motifs, and themes, as well as his attitude towards the poetry of men like Gottfried, Hartmann, Reinmar, and Heinrich von Veldeke.

Gottfried von Strassburg praised Heinrich von Veldeke for the important work he had done in developing German style. In addition to stylistic contributions Veldeke had, through his *Eneide,* spread the literary topos of Ovidian love in Germany. The French, of course, (and not Veldeke) had actually popularized the tradition by liberally appropriating material from the Latin classics. They had come, being grounded in such tradition, to depict love as an overwhelming passion inflicted upon the helpless human heart by the goddess Venus with the help of Cupid or the aid of magic devices like torches and arrows. Hermann of Thuringia, Wolfram's patron, who had been in France, fancied neoclassical literature and he furthered it at home. He supported Veldeke and several other poets working in this vein. Wolfram certainly learned from this imported view of love and indicated quite clearly that he considered Veldeke a "master" in such matters (cf. *P.* 292, 18; 404, 29). However, although Wolfram accepted the passionate aspect characteristic of the Ovidian tradition, he was also concerned with clarifying these passions and raising them to a higher level of control and illumination. In *Parzival* Wolfram quite consciously transmuted both the content and the form of Heinrich's topoi. It is significant, as we shall see, that Wolfram disagreed, in part, with Veldeke's manner of teaching love. Gottfried had, after all, singled out precisely that aspect of Veldeke's poetry for especial praise.[20]

It was Gottfried, too, who named Reinmar of Hagenau as the "lady marshal" of those nightingales who "all know their calling and can express their pining so well in words and song." We remember that Reinmar had been the lyric master of an introspective cult of love. Unlike Reinmar, Wolfram von Eschenbach was not a literary "masochist." He was distinctly activist and could be irascible with those who so consciously cultivated their suffering and "pining." Reinmar was, therefore, an almost predestined target for Wolfram's anger. After all, his preciousness had provoked ironic responses from Walther von der Vogelweide. It is important to recall that Walther and Reinmar had been rivals at the court in Vienna until circumstances forced Walther to leave. Walther's peregrinations eventually brought him north to Thuringia where so many other famous poets gathered. Wolfram must have met him at Hermann's court, and he seems to have been drawn into Walther's quarrel with Reinmar. One of Wolfram's lyric poems, a parody on courtly love, does, in fact, pick up motifs of a song which Walther had directed against Reinmar. As so often, the details, though elusive, help in fixing a personal position in the crosscurrents of literary controversy, and in determining attitudes toward the basic themes of courtly culture.[21]

Wolfram's own attitudes emerge again when we examine his peculiar relationship to Hartmann von Aue. We know that Wolfram was acquainted with Hartmann's *Erec* and *Iwein*, for he refers to both works in his *Parzival*. He refers to *Erec*, for example, while preparing his description of Parzivâl's arrival at the court in Nantes:

> mîn hêr Hartmann von Ouwe,
> frou Ginovêr iwer frouwe
> und iwer hêrre der künc Artûs,
> den kumt ein mîn gast ze hûs.
> bitet hüeten sîn vor spotte.
> ern ist gîge noch diu rotte:
> si sulen ein ander gampel nemn:
> des lâzen sich durch zuht gezemn,
> anders iwer frouwe Enîde
> unt ir muoter Karsnafîde
> werdent durch die mül gezücket
> unde ir lop gebrücket.
> sol ich den munt mit spotte zern,
> ich wil mînen vriunt mit spotte wern.   (*P.* 143, 21–144, 4) *

* "Sir Hartmann von Ouwe! To the house of your Lady Ginover and your lord, King Arthur, a guest of mine is coming. Please to protect

Hartmann had played a decisive role in introducing Arthurian themes to Germany and he must therefore have been considered a sort of representative of the Arthurian ideal. For this reason, Wolfram feels that he must address Hartmann just as Arthur is about to appear in his own narrative for the first time. Wolfram threatens his fellow romancer; he seems to be "afraid" that the barbarian Parzivâl, only recently arrived from the backwoods, will be treated disdainfully by Hartmann's fine heroes. It appears that Wolfram had to take sides with the primitive and unruly boy; he had to defend him against those all too civilized Arthurians. Much of this insight is gained by implication, of course, but references to Hartmann's *Iwein* at least make it clear that Wolfram rejected this romance's rather frivolous treatment of simple decencies and its contorted if gallant attempt to motivate the sudden love of a wife for her husband's killer (cf. *P.* 436, 1 ff).

Important points emerge from this discussion of literary relationships. Wolfram had an uneasy feeling about certain aspects of the traditions purveyed by courtly writers. He was uneasy about the implied symbolic thrust of Veldeke's Ovidian topoi and his implied acceptance of Eros's dominance. He was unimpressed by Reinmar's "esthetic" cultivation of introspective sorrow, and he rejected the stylized elegance and topical frivolity of certain of Hartmann's Arthurian figures. It is perhaps in character, therefore, that Gottfried von Strassburg, Wolfram's antipode, should praise all three writers (Veldeke, Reinmar, and Hartmann) while damning their "rustic" opponent utterly. In *Tristan* Gottfried himself carried the courtly stylistic practices of Veldeke and Hartmann to a point of almost precious affectation, and he celebrated with special genius precisely those facets of courtly tradition which Wolfram had rejected: Eros's triumph, esthetic introspection, "frivolity," and literary elegance.

Wolfram was a product of the land. He was a knight, a ministerial, a layman, a man of piety devoted to the feudal system, and an optimist. He was, above all, well trained in arms and consid-

---

him from mockery there! He is neither a fiddle nor a rote: let them get some other plaything and out of courtesy amuse themselves with that. Or else your Lady Enite and her mother Karsnafite will be put through the mill and have their fame bent down. If I am forced to misuse my mouth for mockery, then with mockery I will defend my friend."

ered "service to the shield" his primary obligation. Poetry was an
avocation for him. Still he appears to have been well versed in
popular genres. He had absorbed that religious teaching which
the clergy aimed at the laity like a great sponge; he was cognizant
of the major literary movements then current in Germany and
had, it would seem, imbibed all the motives and plot lines of
French romance and chanson as well as of certain scientific and
pseudoscientific knowledge. Gottfried was a product of the city.
He was probably a cleric, a scholar perhaps, but certainly an
esthete and surely disinclined to feats of arms—a skeptic, convinced of the rights of the noble of heart to rule this earth, but
resigned to the fact that this cannot be, since the mean must drag
them down—in short a pessimist. Literature was his way of life.
He was versed in music, law, Latin rhetoric, and well acquainted
with the elegant usages and customs of "society." He surely was
well acquainted with both French and Latin literature.

Their romances *Parzival* and *Tristan* project the chasm separat-
ing these two men, the most important narrative poets of the German Middle Ages. Wolfram's hero receives no formal schooling; he
is merely given a great deal of advice haphazardly. In turn, Gottfried's hero learns at an early age the pain of scholarly discipline;
he is sent abroad where he perfects his knowledge of foreign languages, studies books, and plays stringed instruments. Wolfram's
hero is a knight with all his heart and soul, naïve at first but
upright, whereas Gottfried's hero is an efficient but somewhat
reluctant warrior, who is crafty and quite capable of subterfuge.
Wolfram's hero finds fulfillment as king in the castle of the Grail,
surrounded by his wife, family, offspring, and followers, given
over to the service of mankind and standing at the head of a vi-
able political structure, an idealized projection of the feudal
system and knightly orders. But Gottfried's hero finds fulfillment
in the cave of love, alone with Isolde, the wife of another, feasting
only upon her glance, given over to music, song and poetry, surrounded by a rhetorically stylized ideal landscape, a *locus
amoenus,* cast out of a corrupt and scheming court and kingdom;
his only real hope is death.

The literary worlds of Gottfried and Wolfram contradict and
complement each other, demonstrating the realization of two literary modes, both quite different yet perfectly understandable
when viewed in the context of medieval tradition. Gottfried rep-

resents the culmination of an intellectual and facile strain, *vide* his enlightened mockery of medieval faith in ordeals, his elegant parody of the medieval legend's fairy-tale belief in God's happy ending, his daring transposition of mystical, allegorical description to a temple of earthly love, where the bed consecrated to Venus stands at the place of the altar. Wolfram, on the other hand, represents the culmination of a tradition of dynamic faith and simple commitment, nourished by a whole body of legend and myth, perceiving the world and the movement of history as a stage upon which the will of God is revealed and is carried out through institutions devoted to His service.

CHAPTER 3

Parzival: *Composition and Plot*

I *Composition*

WOLFRAM'S *Parzival* is the best preserved work of the medieval *Blütezeit,* the flowering period of German literature around 1200. More than eighty manuscripts and fragments have been discovered, a convincing proof of the romance's popularity during the Middle Ages. Karl Lachmann, one of the great German philologists, produced the first reliable edition of the work in 1833. He dedicated it to three distinguished scholars: Georg Benecke, his teacher in Göttingen, and Jakob and Wilhelm Grimm, his friends and colleagues. It is a tribute to Wolfram that some of the most famous names in German philology are linked with the first serious scholarly efforts to free his *Parzival* from the dross and obscurity of those centuries during which it had been all but forgotten and during which Wolfram's reputation had come to be mistakenly based on a poem he had not even written.[1]

A study of the *Parzival* manuscripts indicates that, beginning with Book V, Wolfram developed the practice of composing in thirty-line segments; from Book V on, the first line of each section of thirty lines is usually distinguished in the better manuscripts by a specially colored or larger letter of the alphabet. Significantly, this line often marks the beginning of a sentence or of a new development in the narrative. The manuscript also gives us reason to divide *Parzival* into "chapters." Such divisions are, for example, marked in the Sankt Gallen manuscript by means of illuminated letters. On the basis of these letters, Lachmann divided *Parzival* into sixteen such "chapters" or "Books" (choosing, however, to ignore some of the evidence because it was in his opinion "unfitting"). Nevertheless, Lachmann's sixteen Books have established themselves, and they do at least offer a standardized and effective tool for discussion and reference. It is an important question whether each segment represents a unit consciously created, possibly for a night's reading. A positive answer to this question would have great significance for our understanding of the structure of the romance.

Wolfram's literary works were produced under difficult circumstances, for he was forced to move about in search of a livelihood. From the comments he makes in *Parzival* we can conclude that, during the composition of Book IV, he was in Wertheim on the Main (*P.* 184, 4). And when writing Book V he was in the Odenwald—at the castle of Wildenberg (*P.* 230, 12–13), whereas, while composing Book VI, he was already at Hermann's court in Thuringia (*P.* 297, 16–18). However, he had evidently left Thuringia when writing Book XIII, since he speaks of the new dances which have just come from there (*P.* 639, 12).

Wolfram's unsettled life was certainly not conducive to continuous literary effort, and his *Parzival* was produced at an uneven pace. By cataloguing and comparing the changes in Wolfram's use of rhyme words,[2] vocabulary, formulae,[3] and metrical types,[4] scholars have been able to uncover some details of the writing process. There is a certain amount of agreement as far as the broader outlines are concerned. There was, for example, a longer pause after the completion of Book VI. This would fit well with other evidence. At the end of Book VI (*P.* 337, 23 ff.), Wolfram displays a certain unwillingness to continue his tale. In Book VII he refers to the destructiveness of the Erfurt siege, a contemporary event important to the Thuringians. This siege must have taken place some time after the conclusion of Book VI. Now a comparison of Wolfram's work with manuscripts of Chrestien's *Perceval* (Wolfram's French source) indicates that Wolfram used a different manuscript of *Perceval* after he completed Book VI.[5] The siege (in which Wolfram probably took part as a member of the Thuringian army) and a lost manuscript could, therefore, have caused the interruption which scholars posit on the basis of philological analysis.

An examination of Wirnt von Gravenberg's *Wigalois* shows that Wirnt was acquainted with Books I to VI of *Parzival* when he wrote his own work.[6] This would seem to prove that a "first edition" of *Parzival*, consisting only of the first six Books, was in circulation before Wolfram completed the tale. It is interesting that *P.* 336 and 337 (two thirty-line sections at the end of Book VI) are lacking in major manuscripts of the G tradition. These two thirty-line sections disperse the major characters of the romance, sum up the positive features of the heroines of the tale, and conclude with an indication on the author's part of his unwillingness to continue the story. The two sections, a perfect conclusion in themselves, may have been added after Wolfram had realized that he could not, for the time being, continue writing. They formed a temporary "epilogue" to his "first edition." The publication of the first six Books (in 1203?) may, in turn, have been followed by other partial publications (and revisions?). At least there would seem to have been pauses between Books VIII and IX, XIII and XIV, XIV and XV .

A very significant question touching upon the problem of order of composition (which is connected with the question of Wolfram's originality) is that of the chronology of Books I and II. There are various theories according to which these Books were written either first, i.e., in normal order, at the end, after all the other books had been completed, or at another point along the way. If we accept the theory that Books I and II were essentially Wolfram's original creation (there is no real counterpart to I and II in Chrestien's *Perceval*), the most satisfying theory would be that Books I and II were written, at the earliest, after the completion of Books III to VI. The major argument against this thesis is that Wolfram does not begin to compose in verse groups of thirty lines until Book V; if Books I and II had been written after Book VI, one would expect them to have been composed in thirty-line groups also. However, if we begin to count from the end of Book II, that is from *P.* 114, 4, omitting *P.* 69, 29–70, 6 (which have always been considered an interpolation), we discover that Book II consists of fifty-five thirty-line sections. If we count from the end of Book I (*P.* 58, 26), we arrive (after fifty-four thirty-line sections) at *P.* 4, 27 (the real beginning of Book I).[7] From this point of view, then, Books I and II could have been written after Wolfram had finished Books III to VI. But the situation is complicated and cannot be conclusively resolved.[8]

II *Plot*

The Prologue to *Parzival* (*P.* 1, 1–4, 26) was famous, evidently as early as Wolfram's own times, for its "dicing terms." In it Wolfram seems to throw concepts and imagery together, haphazardly.

The Prologue is characterized by abrupt transitions, and by a lack of coordinating or subordinating words.

Book I (*P*. 4, 27–58, 26). At the end of the Prologue, the poet states:

> den ich hie zuo hân erkorn,
> er ist maereshalp noch ungeborn,
> dem man dirre âventiure giht,
> und wunders vil des dran geschiht. (*P*. 4, 23–26) *

Literary tradition offered the option of a *Vorgeschichte* devoted to the parents of the hero. Accordingly Book I begins to relate the story of Parzivâl's father, Gahmuret. Driven by an inner urge, this young nobleman sets out in search of love and fame. His ambition will allow him to serve no other but the most powerful man on earth, a heathen, "Baruc of Baldac." As a knight errant, Gahmuret wanders through the Arab world, "Morroch," "Persîâ," "Dâmasc," and "Arâbî." He offers his help in "Zazamanc" and saves its queen, a Mooress, Belakâne. It is Gahmuret's nature to love, and he marries the black lady he has rescued, but his craving for adventure will not let him rest. Secretly he provisions his ship and steals away, leaving his heathen wife pregnant. A letter discloses Gahmuret's origins. He is of the house of "Anchouwe" (Anjou?), related to Arthur, and descended from an ancestor who had mated with a fairy in some magic other-world. Sorrowing, the faithful Belekâne gives birth to a son, Feirefîz, a child that is speckled black and white, like a magpie.

Book II (*P*. 58, 27–114, 4). Gahmuret travels by sea and land, arriving finally at Kanvoleis, where a tourney has been proclaimed. Gahmuret is victor in the joustings and wins the hand of Queen Herzeloyde. She demands her right of him, but he resists, proclaiming his loyalty to another lady, the queen of France, and to his beautiful black wife, Belakâne. Herzeloyde appeals to a Court of Love, and judgment is proclaimed in her favor. It is May, and that fairy ancestry stirs the blood of Gahmuret. Again he cannot resist his inner urge. He surrenders to Herzeloyde with the stipulation that she does not interfere with his adventuring.

---

* "The one whom I have thus chosen is, story-wise, as yet unborn, he of whom this adventure tells and to whom many marvels there befall."

Their happiness together is short-lived, however. Gahmuret is wounded in the head by a lance and dies fighting for his lord, "Baruc of Baldac." Herzeloyde faints at the news of his end, then gives birth to a son of great size, Parzivâl:

> hiest der âventiure wurf gespilt,
> und ir begin ist gezilt:
> wand er ist alrêrst geborn,
> dem diz maere wart erkorn. (*P.* 112, 9–12)*

Selbstverteidigung (*P. 114, 5–116, 4*). This *"Self-defense"* (or *Apologia*) is composed of two thirty-line segments. It is inserted between Books II and III and begins: "Swer nu wîben sprichet baz, / deiswâr daz lâze ich âne haz" (*P.* 114, 5–6).† Since Wolfram has ended Book II and begins Book III by praising Herzeloyde and her *triuwe* (loving faithfulness), this digression would not be badly placed. (It has been argued, however, that it was actually intended to augment the Prologue.) In these sixty lines, Wolfram refers to his quarrel with a woman and to the fact that he has incurred the displeasure of the ladies at the court:

> ich bin Wolfram von Eschenbach,
> unt kan ein teil mit sange,
> unt bin ein habendiu zange
> mînen zorn gein einem wîbe:
> diu hât mîme lîbe
> erboten solhe missetât,
> ine hân si hazzens keinen rât.
> dar umb hân ich der andern haz. (*P.* 114, 12–19)‡

The insertion contains a humorous and impassioned defense of the poet's own nature. He is a man of action and not of words. A woman would be mad if she were to love him for his poetry rather

* "Herewith this adventure's dice are cast and its beginning determined, for only now has he been born to whom this tale is devoted."
† "If there is anyone who praises women better than I, I will surely not be one to hold it against him."
‡ "I am Wolfram von Eschenbach, and I know a thing or two about poetry, and I am a tongs at holding my anger against a woman. This one has offered me such an offense that I cannot do other than hate her. On account of this the others hate *me*."

than for his playing for high stakes with shield and spear. The poet's story is not a "book." He does not know a single "letter of the alphabet." The lines *P. 115, 5–7*, in which Wolfram refers to a man's excessive praise of his lady—"she *checkmates* other women" —would seem to refer to Reinmar of Hagenau. At least Reinmar had written a poem using precisely this turn of phrase.

Book III (P. 116, 5–179, 12). Herzeloyde has fled to the wilderness of Soltâne, taking with her Parzivâl and a few servants. She wishes to raise her son far from the court and keep him ignorant of knightly ways in order to save him from ending as his father did. But Gahmuret's *art*, the qualities he has inherited from Gahmuret, move Parzivâl's heart in a way incomprehensible to him. His breast swells with strange emotions and longing disturbs his innocent sense of peace. In simple terms his mother tells him of life, of God who is brighter than the day, who became man, who is *triuwe* ("loving," "faithful"), and who has always helped men. She also tells him of the devil who is black and *untriuwe*, and warns him: "Turn from the devil and from the inconstancy of *zwîvel*, from the inconstancy of doubt, despair."

Herzeloyde cannot shield her son from his destiny. One day Parzivâl comes upon knights of Arthur's court riding through the woods. Their armor shines brightly, and, remembering the words of his mother that God is light, he worships them as God. From the knights he learns of Arthur's court and cannot be restrained. He must become a knight himself. Herzeloyde dresses her son in fool's clothing, hoping that he will be badly used and come running back to her. Her legacy to him is the counsel that he should avoid dark paths, greet all the world, take advice from a gray, wise man who can teach him *zuht* ("courtly form"), and take a good woman's ring and kiss. Parzivâl rides off at the break of the next day, intent upon his way. His mother falls to the ground, dead of a broken heart.

Heeding his mother's advice (which is rooted in the world of the fairy tale) the young fool, a true fairy-tale figure, carries out her instructions with a single-minded literalness. He rides in the sun and comes upon a gaily-colored tent placed upon a meadow. Inside, asleep, is the fair Jeschûte. Parzivâl takes her ring and a kiss (his interpretation of his mother's instructions) and moves on. Jeschûte's husband, Orilus, a proud and jealous knight, returns, sees Parzivâl's tracks, and suspects the very worst. "We will

not eat, sleep and drink together," Orilus says, "until I have found
and punished the intruder." Parzivâl, unwitting and well-
meaning, pushes on to Arthur's court at Nantes. On the way he
finds a maiden in the forest, sadly fondling a dead knight. It is
Sigûne, his cousin. She recognizes him and tells him: "In truth,
your name is Parzival which signifies '*right through the middle.*'"
She tells him that the slain prince, Schîânatulander, has died at
the hands of Orilus, while defending Parzivâl's lands. Parzivâl
grieves for her and promises revenge.

As the fool approaches Arthur's city, he comes upon the Red
Knight, Ither, who has challenged the Round Table and waits before the gates. Ither greets Parzivâl courteously and sends him
into Nantes with a message. Parzivâl, "awkward as a crane," impa-
tiently demands Ither's armor from Arthur and, when his wish has
been reluctantly granted, storms from the court. Cunnewâre
(who was never to laugh) and Antanor (who was never to speak
—until he who was to win the highest honor had come riding to
the court) laugh and speak. Keye, the impulsive seneschal, beats
both the knight and the lady soundly for bestowing their prophecy on such an unlikely candidate as the bumpkin Parzivâl. But
Parzivâl rides to claim his prize. He kills the unsuspecting Ither
with a javelin throw, tears the costly armor from his body, and
leaves Nantes, awkwardly, with shield flapping, a fool's habit beneath his mail.

Riding at incredible speed, Parzivâl comes to the castle of Gurnemanz. A gray sage, Gurnemanz puts away Parzivâl's fool's garb
and proceeds to teach him the rules of courtly conduct, of *zuht,*
and the ways of knightly combat. One part of Gurnemanz's counsel, "Do not ask too many questions," followed later with literal-
mindedness, is to have fateful consequences.

Book IV (*P. 179, 13–223, 30*). Parzivâl has left Gurnemanz's
castle and, seeking trackless paths, rides through wild, high mountains. He finds the city of Pelrapeire, besieged by Clâmidê, who
wants to take the city and the love of its young queen, Condwîrâmûrs, by force. Parzivâl knocks at a city gate, enters and is
brought into the presence of Condwîrâmûrs:

> an der got wunsches niht vergaz
> (diu was des landes frouwe),
> als von dem süezen touwe

> diu rôse ûz ir bälgelîn
> blecket niuwen werden schîn,
> der beidiu wîz ist unde rôt.
> daz fuogte ir gaste grôze nôt.
> sîn manlîch zuht was im sô ganz,
> sît in der werde Gurnamanz
> von sîner tumpheit geschiet
> unde im vrâgen widerriet,
> ez enwaere bescheidenlîche:
> bî der küneginne rîche
> saz sîn munt gar âne wort.   (*P.* 188, 8–21)*

In his simplicity Parzivâl follows the letter of Gurnemanz's law. Parzivâl is naïve but well-meaning. He offers the beautiful maiden his help and eventually defeats Clâmidê. He falls in love with, and marries, Condwîrâmûrs. Both Parzivâl and Condwîrâmûrs are innocent. She becomes his virgin bride and after the first night ties on the headdress of a matron, although the marriage has not been consummated:

> si wâren mit ein ander sô,
> daz si durch liebe wâren vrô,
> zwên tage unt die dritten naht.
> von im dicke wart gedâht
> umbevâhens, daz sîn muoter riet:
> Gurnemanz im ouch underschiet,
> man und wîp waern al ein.
> si vlâhten arm unde bein.
> ob ichz iu sagen müeze,
> er vant daz nâhe süeze.   (*P.* 202, 29–203, 8)†

* ". . . In *her* God had not omitted any wish, she was mistress of the land, and like the rose washed with the sweet dew that from its bud sends forth its new and noble glow, red and white together. This caused her guest great perplexity. For his manly courtesy was so perfect since the worthy Gurnemanz had cured him of his simplicity and counseled him against questions, unless they were discreet ones, that he sat there with that noble queen without opening his mouth to speak a word, . . ."

† "Two days and the third night they were happy with one another in their affection. To him there often came the thought of embracing her, as his mother had counseled him—and Gurnemanz too had explained to him that man and wife are one. And so they entwined arms and legs, if I may be allowed to tell you so, and he found the closeness sweet."

Book V (P. 224, 1–279, 30). Parzivâl sets out once more, this time to see how his mother fares. Again he rides through rugged country, over fallen trees and through marshy lands. He finds a lake and, in a boat, a fisherman with rich apparel who tells him the way to an awesome castle. It is a place strangely melancholy yet luxuriously appointed in every way. Parzivâl is led into the great hall, where an odd ritual begins. Finally a queen enters:

> ûf einem grüenen achmardî
> truoc si den wunsch von pardîs,
> bêde wurzeln unde rîs.
> daz was ein dinc, daz hiez der Grâl,
> erden wunsches überwal.
> Repanse de schoy si hiez,
> die sich der grâl tragen liez.
> der grâl was von sölher art:
> wol muoser kiusche sîn bewart
> diu sîn ze rehte solde pflegen:
> diu muose valsches sich bewegen.   (*P.* 235, 20–30) *

The whole company is served from the Grail which provides all manner of food and drink. The lord of the castle, the Fisher King, seems to be gravely ill, but he treats Parzivâl with great ceremony and gives him a sword. Parzivâl watches intently and would like to inquire about the meaning of what he sees, but, following Gurnemanz's advice, he refrains from doing so. At this point, Wolfram injects his own comment into the narrative:

> ôwê daz er niht vrâgte dô!
> des pin ich vür in noch unvrô.
> wan do erz enpfienc in sîne hant,
> dô was er vrâgens mit ermant.
> och riwet mich sîn süezer wirt,
> den ungenânde niht verbirt,
> des im von vrâgn nu waere rât.   (*P.* 240, 3–9) †

* "Upon a deep green achmardi [precious cloth] she bore the perfection of Paradise, both root and branch. That was a thing called the Grail, which surpasses all earthly perfection. Repanse de Schoye was the name of her whom the Grail permitted to be its bearer. Such was the nature of the Grail that she who watched over it had to preserve her purity and renounce all falsity."

† "Alas that he did not ask the question then! I still sorrow for him on

Parzivâl is shown to his room. He lies richly bedded, but his sleep is troubled by heavy dreams, and he awakens, his body in a sweat, to find the castle deserted. He runs screaming to his horse. In a passion of grief and anger he leaves the castle, determined to find his host and repay his kindness, but loses the track he is following in the forest. He hears lamentation and discovers a maiden beneath a linden tree, holding a knight dead and embalmed in her arms. The maiden is Sigûne.

She realizes that Parzivâl has been at the Grail Castle, Munsalvaesche, and prophesies that he can win riches, honor, and power, but only by asking the question. When she learns that he has failed to do so, she curses him mercilessly:

> "iuch solt iur wirt erbarmet hân,
> an dem got wunder hât getân,
> und het gevrâget sîner nôt.
> ir lebt, und sît an saelden tôt."   (*P.* 255, 17–20) *

Parzivâl promises to atone for anything he has done, leaves Sigûne, and actually repairs one of his first wrongs. He chances upon Jeschûte and Orilus and, by force of arms, wins back Orilus's favor for Jeschûte, then swears an oath that she had not willingly given up her ring and kiss on that fateful day when he found her in the tent:

> "ich was ein tôre und niht ein man,
> gewahsen niht pî witzen.
> vil weinens, dâ bî switzen
> mit jâmer dolte vil ir lîp.
> si ist benamn ein unschuldic wip."   (*P.* 269, 24–28) †

---

that account. For when the sword was put into his hand, it was a sign that he should ask. And I pity too his sweet host whom God's displeasure does not spare and who could have been freed from it by a question."

* " 'You should have felt pity for your host, on whom God has wrought such terrible wonders, and have asked the cause of his suffering. You live, and yet are dead to happiness.' "

† " 'I was a fool then, not a man, and not yet grown to wisdom. Many tears did she shed, and she sweat in anguish at what she suffered there. She is truly an innocent woman.' "

Book VI (*P. 280, 1–337, 30*). Arthur has gone in search of Parzivâl and camps at Plimizoel. Athough it is Pentecost, snow has
fallen. A goose, struck by a hunting falcon, has left three drops of
red blood on the snow. Parzivâl chances upon the blood drops,
sees in them an image of Condwîrâmûrs, and, filled with longing,
falls into a trance. Arthur's knights, glimpsing him before the
camp, interpret his presence as a challenge and are concerned
about their honor. First Segramors, and then Keye, ride a joust
against him, and both are felled, Keye with broken limbs. Gâwân,
the courtly paragon, determines to win the strange knight with
reason; he goes up to him, sees the blood drops, and, wise in the
ways of love, drops a cloak over them, thus freeing Parzivâl from
their magic power.

Parzivâl is led in triumph to Arthur and made a member of the
Table Round. At this point, the culmination of Parzivâl's triumph
in the courtly world, disaster strikes. Cundrìe, the Grail Messenger, comes riding to the camp, crying:

> "ir vederangl, ir nâtern zan!
> iu gap iedoch der wirt ein swert,
> des iwer wirde wart nie wert:
> da erwarb iu swîgen sünden zil.
> ir sît der hellehirten spil.
> gunêrter lîp, hêr Parzivâl!
> ir sâht ouch vür iuch tragen den grâl,
> und snidnde silbr und bluotic sper.
> ir fröuden letze, ir trûrens werl!"   (*P. 316, 20–28*) *

Parzivâl, in the midst of honor, is suddenly dishonored. Torn by
grief and rage, uncomprehending, and convinced of his own innocence and good will, he renounces God:

> "ich was im diens undertân,
> sît ich genâden mich versan.
> nu wil i'm dienst widersagn:
> hât er haz, den wil ich tragn."   (*P. 332, 5–8*) †

* " 'You baited lure! You adder's fang! Your host gave you a sword, of
which you were never worthy. Your silence earned you there the sin
supreme. You are the sport of the shepherds of hell. Dishonored are
you, Sir Parzival. Yet you saw the Grail borne before you and the silver
knives and the bloody spear. You death of joy and bestowal of grief.' "
† " 'I was in His service, since I hoped to receive His grace. But now I
shall renounce His service, and if He hates me, that hate I will bear.' "

In this moment of crisis, Gâwân serves as a parallel and as a contrast to Parzivâl. Like him, he receives a public slur that tarnishes his reputation, for Kingrimursel arrives at court and cries out:

> "daz ist hie hêr Gâwân,
>
> . . . .
> unprîs sîn het aldâ gewalt,
> dô in sîn gir dar zuo vertruoc,
> ime gruozer mînen hêrren sluoc." (*P.* 321, 5–10)*

Gâwân denies Kingrimursel's charge, but without surrendering to rage. He arms himself and leaves to prove his innocence in trial by combat. Parzivâl sets out to seek the Grail.

Books VII, VIII, X, XI, XII, and XIII. These books concern themselves essentially with Gâwân, and Parzivâl appears only intermittently.

Book VII (*P.* 338, 1–397, 30). Gâwân, on his way to defend his reputation in combat with Kingrimursel, becomes involved, against his will, in the siege of Bêârosche. As the knight of Obilôt, a little girl who plays at courtly love as she would at dolls, Gâwân defeats Meljanz and raises the siege of the city. With Gâwân's help Meljanz and Obîe (Obilôt's older and evil-tempered sister) are brought together. The lovers' quarrel (which had separated the two and led to the campaign) is solved and a betrothal announced. Obilôt is saddened by Gâwân's departure.

Book VIII (*P.* 398, 1–432, 30). At Ascalûn, the place appointed for the trial by combat, Gâwân is surprised in a delicate situation with the seductive Antikonîe, daughter of the king allegedly murdered by him. The two are besieged in a bedroom and, after a mock-heroic battle, Gâwân is allowed to proceed, on the condition that he seek the Grail. Again he leaves a saddened female behind.

Book IX (*P.* 433, 1–502, 30). Parzivâl, riding through pathless wastes, has lost track of time but still seeks the Grail. He finds a hermitage and, in it, kneeling beside a coffin, Sigûne. Hearing that Munsalvaesche is near, he will not stay, pushes on and chances upon a pilgrim, a knight in gray. Since it is Good Friday, the Gray

---

* " 'It is Sir Gawan here. . . . Dishonor ruled him then when base desire misled him to kill my lord as he gave him greeting.' "

Knight, Kahenîs, is surprised to find Parzivâl armed. He speaks of the love of God who died on the cross for mankind. Parzivâl, moved now to repentance, entrusts himself to divine power, wishing to test God's capacity to help. He gives his horse its head and is taken straight to Trevrezent, his uncle and the brother of Anfortas (the suffering King of the Grail Castle).

Parzivâl is filled with a new awareness and greets Trevrezent with these words: "Sir, now give me counsel. I am a man who has sinned." In the time Parzivâl spends with Trevrezent he learns that Ither (whom he had slain) was of his own flesh and blood, and that his own mother (who is Trevrezent's sister) had died because of him. He discovers that Anfortas was suffering from a poisoned wound sustained in pursuing the illicit love of a woman (Orgelûse). He learns of the ways of God, of original sin and the fall of the angels, of the mysteries of the Grail itself, and of the chaste and humble brotherhood of Munsalvaesche:

> "jane mac den grâl nieman bejagn,
> wan der ze himel ist sô bekant
> daz er zem grâle sî benant.
> des muoz ich vome grâle jehn:
> ich weizz und hânz vür wâr gesehn."   (P. 468, 12–16) *

Parzivâl realizes that he has been driven, these long years, by blind rage and rebellious pride. He comes to understand that his doubt of God's grace was a passion, a sort of madness. As Parzivâl leaves the hermitage, filled with a new peace, Trevrezent reassures him:

> . . . "gip mir dîn sünde her:
> vor gote ich bin dîn wandels wer.
> und leist als ich dir hân gesagt:
> belîp des willen unverzagt."   (P. 502, 25–28) †

---

* " '. . . no man can ever win the Grail unless he is known in heaven and he be called by name to the Grail. This I must tell you about the Grail, for I know it to be so and have seen it for myself.' "

† " 'Give your sins to me. In the sight of God, I am the guaranty for your atonement. And now do as I have bidden you, and follow that course undaunted.' "

Book X (*P. 503, 1–552, 30*). In spite of dire prophecy, Gâwân takes up the service of Orgelûse, a capricious and seemingly hardhearted lady, who has driven many champions (among them Anfortas) to their doom. Gâwân is hopelessly in love and, having had a series of misadventures, comes with this haughty beauty to the foot of "Schastel marveile." Orgelûse cruelly laughs at all his suffering.

Book XI (*P. 553, 1–582, 30*). Four hundred ladies are imprisoned in the "Castle of Marvels" by the evil sorcerer Clinschor. Gâwân successfully undergoes the test of the Marvelous Bed and frees the women. Among them are his grandmother, mother, and sister.

Book XII (*P. 583, 1–626, 30*). Gâwân fetches a chaplet from the tree in the garden of fearsome Gramoflanz. Gramoflanz had killed Cidegast, Orgelûse's beloved. The grief over his death had made her mad, and, in her suffering, she had driven knight after knight to fight with Gramoflanz. Gâwân's deed wins him her love.

Book XIII (*P. 627, 1–678, 30*). Gâwân and Orgelûse are married. A messenger from Gâwân brings Arthur with all his knights and ladies to the Castle of Marvels.

Book XIV (*P. 679, 1–733, 30*). Parzivâl and Gâwân, with visors closed, not recognizing each other, meet in combat. Parzivâl is on the verge of defeating Gâwân when recognition comes and the battle stops. Parzivâl is taken in triumph to the Arthurian court, and now his reputation in this world seems greater than ever. A great festival ensues and culminates in a series of weddings. But torn by grief for the Grail and longing for Condwîrâmûrs, Parzivâl steals away. His sorrow has no place in this joyous atmosphere.

Book XV (*P. 734, 1–786, 30*). Parzivâl, riding in a bright glade, encounters a heathen richly armed. This unbaptized man's ship had anchored in a bay near the forest. Seeking adventure, he had left his army of Moors and Saracens behind. Parzivâl and the unknown knight see each other from afar and charge their horses. The battle, fought first on horseback, then on foot, is undecided until, at its climax, Parzivâl's sword breaks apart:

> got des niht langer ruochte,
> daz Parzivâl daz rê nemen

> in sîner hende solde zemen:
> daz swert er Ithêre nam,
> als sîner tumpheit dô wol zam.   (P. 744, 14–18) *

The heathen, seeing that his opponent is helpless, throws his sword away and discloses his identity. He is Feirefîz, the speckled son of Gahmuret and Belakâne, and thus Parzivâl's half-brother. The two journey to King Arthur's camp. Amid general rejoicing, Cundrîe, the messenger of the Grail, arrives and proclaims that the Grail's epitaph has pronounced that Parzivâl is to be king of Munsalvaesche after all.

Book XVI (*P. 787, 1–827, 30*). Parzivâl arrives at the Grail castle with Feirefîz. He kneels in prayer, then asks the question of compassion. Anfortas's miraculous cure is immediately effected:

> . . . der Lazarum bat ûf stên,
> der selbe half daz Anfortas
> wart gesunt unt wol genas.   (P. 796, 2–4) †

Parzivâl rides to meet Condwîrâmûrs, who is being brought toward Munsalvaesche, and comes upon the astonished Trevrezent, who says:

> "groezer wunder selten ie geschach,
> sît ir ab got erzürnet hât
> daz sîn endelôsiu Trinitât
> iwers willen werhaft worden ist."   (P. 798, 2–5) ‡

Parzivâl and Condwîrâmûrs are reunited. They all return to Munsalvaesche, and there Feirefîz is baptized, for he wishes to marry Repanse de Schoye, the keeper of the Grail. The newly married couple travels to Feirefîz's heathen kingdom, where one day Repanse is to give birth to a son named John, who will Christian-

---

* "God would not allow corpse robbing to thrive in Parzival's hand, for this was the sword he had taken from Ither, as then befitted his simplicity."

† ". . . Who bade Lazarus arise, the Same gave help that Anfortas was healed and made well again."

‡ " 'Greater miracle has seldom come to pass, for you forced God by defiance to make His infinite Trinity grant your will.' "

ize the East. Wolfram concludes with this summary of his accomplishment:

> sîniu kint, sîn hôch geslehte
> hân ich iu benennet rehte,
> Parzivâls, den ich hân brâht
> dar sîn doch saelde het erdâht.
> swes lebn sich sô verendet,
> daz got niht wirt gepfendet
> der sêle durch des lîbes schulde,
> und der doch der werlde hulde
> behalten kan mit werdekeit,
> daz ist ein nütziu arbeit.   (*P*. 827, 15–24) *

* "His children and his high race I have rightly named for you, Parzival's I mean, whom I brought to the place which, in spite of everything, his blessedness had destined for him. A life so concluded that God is not robbed of the soul through fault of the body, and which can obtain the world's favor with dignity, *that* is a worthy work."

CHAPTER 4

Parzival: *Sources*

W OLFRAM informs us that the known author of the *Conte del Gral*, Chrestien de Troyes, failed to tell his tale of the Grail correctly. A Provençal named Kyot rendered the story in the proper manner, he says; what is more, Kyot, in contrast to Chrestien, told his tale to the very end (*P*. 827, 1–11). Unfortunately, scholars have been unable to identify Kyot. Many consider him a fictitious character, since the most satisfactory attempts at pinpointing Wolfram's source have been those which fall back upon a comparison between Wolfram's *Parzival* and Chrestien's *Conte;* such studies leave little doubt that Wolfram knew and used some form of Chrestien's romance.[1] But Chrestien's *Perceval* does not contain the story to which Wolfram devotes the first two Books of *Parzival*, nor did Chrestien ever conclude the work in question, as Wolfram himself indicates. Chrestien's *Perceval* breaks off at a point which would correspond to the middle of Book XIII in Wolfram's poem (the scene in which Gâwân's messenger arrives at Arthur's court).

I *Books I and II, Books XIII–XVI*

Supplying a beginning and an end to *Perceval* was a task which taxed the imagination of poets who carried on after Chrestien's death. In two manuscripts (L and P) of the French Continuations we find a Prologue which purports to give the story of Perceval's father. The French Prologue calls the hero's father Bliocadran—not Gahmuret—but proceeds, in some other respects, in rather familiar fashion: although his wife is with child, Bliocadran cannot be persuaded to give up tourneying and dies after being wounded in the head by a lance. His pregnant wife faints at the news of his untimely end and gives birth to a baby boy. She seeks refuge in the woods in order to save this son from his father's fate.

Wolfram may have had access to this Prologue, directly or indirectly.

The French story of Bliocadran cannot, however, completely account for Wolfram's complex *Vorgeschichte*. Wolfram (or his alternate source) must have had access to still other "information." It is believed that the Dutch poem *Moraien* might have provided inspiration for the first Book of *Parzival*, the French *Joufrois* for the second,[2] and the German *Eneide* for both.[3] *Moraien*, a work of the fourteenth century (based on a French source known in some earlier form to Wolfram or Kyot?), tells of Walewein's (and Lancelot's) search for Perceval. In the course of their quest, the two meet a strange knight, a Moor. The Moor is Perceval's nephew; his father had had a love affair with a black heatheness but had deserted her. The French poem *Joufrois* (written at the end of the twelfth or the beginning of the thirteenth century) could also have contributed something to Wolfram's version: at least the German poet's description of Gahmuret's entry into Kanvoleis, of his tent beneath Herzeloyde's castle, and of his sorrow at the death of Galoes seems to have been written in imitation of certain features of the French adventure. Finally, there is the *Eneide* of Heinrich von Veldeke, the story of a knight who wins a lady in Africa, deserts her, and wins a second wife (to whom he remains faithful) in another land; this tale might have supplied the general outline for most of Books I and II and did, in any case, serve as the source for some smaller details: Belakâne's harbor city is modeled on Dîdô's harbor city as described in Veldeke's work, and Gahmurets's burial on that of Kamille and Pallas.[4]

Books I and II of *Parzival* are carefully integrated into the body of the German tale. Wolfram himself could, of course, have combined all sources as effectively as Kyot. Stories about adventurous journeys and successful courtships of a bride in the East were favorite themes of "minstrel" poetry. The oriental scenery would require no special explanation, as Wolfram lived in an age of Crusades. More than one of his benefactors had participated in the wars, and the Western world was full of stories about Saladin (who might have furnished the model for Gahmuret's heathen lord). It could also have been Wolfram himself who worked out the details of the Gahmuret figure, inspired perhaps by the person of Richard the Lion-Hearted, Saladin's flamboyant adversary.

There are at least some very loose similarities between Parzivâl's father and that rash hero of the Crusades. Both Gahmuret and Richard stem from the house of Anjou and trace their lineage back to the fairies. After the death of his elder brother Gandîn, Gahmuret becomes ruler of Anschouwe, Waleis, and Norgals, and Richard ruler of Anjou, South Wales, and North Wales after the death of his elder brother Henry. Both Gahmuret and Richard are friendly with Mohammedan princes; both die tragically and unexpectedly. During the composition of part of *Parzival*, Richard was held prisoner by the German Emperor Henry VI at Trifels castle in the Palatinate. Some of Wolfram's patrons certainly had personal contact with Richard. Was Wolfram perhaps attempting to interpret contemporary issues by incorporating representative personae into the "myth" of his poem? Does Gahmuret-Richard serve as a type of courtly, worldly adventurer, and Baruc-Saladin as that of noble heathen? Or did Wolfram take over material already formed by Kyot? [5]

Like Books I and II, Books XIII to XVI cannot be shown to be the product of a single source. The conclusion to the work could have derived, in some fashion, from the French continuation of *Perceval* (with which Wolfram's version agrees in some details). But inspiration could also have come from Hartmann's *Iwein*, a work known to Wolfram.[6] The structural principles of the Arthurian romance of the type represented by Iwein required that, at the conclusion of the tale, the hero prove his powers by battling that Arthurian paragon, Gawain. In keeping with the "rules," the hero was to be acclaimed by Arthur and his court. This is, as we have seen, precisely what happens towards the end of Wolfram's *Parzival*. Furthermore, the battle of Parzivâl with his half-brother Feirefîz (which follows the contest with Gâwân, and which helps Wolfram to join the last two Books with the first two), appears to have been inspired by the French *Ipomedon*. The parallels which *Ipomedon* offers are fairly convincing. In the French poem, two half-brothers meet and fight near the sea. The one, whose armor is rich, has ridden out alone, leaving his army close behind. The battle is joined after the brothers have seen each other from afar. One of them loses the power to defend himself; the other then throws away his sword. The combatants remove their helmets, tell each other their adventures, and go off together.

When we compare Wolfram's *Parzival* with Chrestien's *Perce-*

val, it strikes us that the German version grows increasingly independent in the later Books. Wolfram—who surely must have known that Chrestien had died without finishing his work—may have realized, at some point along the way, that he would have to find a conclusion of his own. He may have used Chrestien at first but then have distanced himself from him as his own conclusion (invented or suggested by other works) became increasingly clear. It was, above all the Grail sphere which had, in Chrestien's *Perceval*, remained something of an unsolved puzzle. A new version would be required to remedy this situation if the tale was to conclude successfully. It was in this mysterious other-world beyond the Arthurian court that the last strands of the story would have to be joined. Wolfram's *Parzival* does give greater weight to the Grail complex by developing the lineage of the Grail family, and by supplying a wealth of new information about the Grail itself, about its origins and functions, and about the society of knights and ladies who serve it.

II *The Grail and Its Sources*

Chrestien's Grail is a large, broad vessel decorated with precious stones, whereas Wolfram's Grail is itself a precious stone—a conception absolutely unique in the known body of literature on the sacred talisman. The German poet's version of the Grail complex is, in fact, characterized by a whole host of changes and additions which both contradict and exceed anything to be found in Chrestien's work.

Most of the details concerning Wolfram's Grail and the Grail Society are given in Book IX (although there is important information to be found in Books V and XVI also). According to Wolfram, the Grail is stored in a temple and brought forth upon the occasion of special festivals (*P*. 807, 16–17). It can be carried only by a pure virgin; an unworthy person cannot move it from the spot. The Grail makes known its wishes and appoints its servants by means of an epitaph which appears and disappears mysteriously upon the stone (*P*. 470, 21–24; 470, 28–30). It is of such a nature that it cannot be seen by the unbaptized (*P*. 813, 17–211). The mysterious, manifold powers of the Grail derive from a host laid upon it once a year, on Good Friday, by a dove that descends from, and returns to, heaven (*P*. 469, 29–470, 20). It has the function of a "horn of plenty," dispensing food and drink of all sorts to the members of the Society of the Grail (*P.* 238, 8–24). Through the power of the stone, the Phoenix is consumed and restored (*P.* 469, 8–13). A man who looks upon the Grail cannot die during the week after, the Grail giving him youth and health (*P.* 469, 14–28). It cannot be found by deliberate search but must be come upon unknowingly (*P.* 250, 26–30).

The Grail was, at one time, guarded by neutral angels, i.e., by those angels who stood neither on the side of God nor on that of Lucifer in the first rebellion (*P.* 471, 15 ff.). It later passed from the care of the neutral angels into that of a chosen group of human beings (*P.* 454, 27–30), the family of Mazadân. Mazadân gave the Grail to Titurel, Titurel to Frimutel, and Frimutel to Anfortas (*P.* 455, 13–19). In this family lies the Kingship over the Grail and the Grail Society. When he was the King of the Grail, Anfortas assigned the Grail Society the dove as its symbol (*P.* 474, 5–8). The King of the Grail is permitted to have a wife (*P.* 495, 9–12), but if he seeks the love of a woman other than the one granted him by the epitaph on the Grail, he must suffer for his disobedience (*P.* 478, 13–16). The members of the Grail Society, who are knights, are called *templeise* (knights of the "temple"? Templars?) (*P.* 468, 28) and fight their battles as penance for their sins (*P.* 468, 29–30). Those chosen for service in the Society of the Grail, both male and female, are called by the epitaph upon the Grail (*P.* 470, 24–27). The chosen ones come as children to the Grail Castle. They come from families both rich and poor, and from many lands (*P.* 471, 1–9). The members of the Grail Society are distinguished by their humility (*P.* 473, 4) and purity (*P.* 493, 24). They are at times sent into various countries in order to rule there (*P.* 494, 5–12). From the family of the Grail spring Lohengrin, the Swan Knight, and Prester John, a legendary Christian King of the East.

These are the details which the German poem offers in addition to, or in contradiction of, Chrestien. The changes and additions which Wolfram's version makes in the ceremonies surrounding the Grail are less striking, perhaps, but far from unimportant. The Grail ceremony, as described in Chrestien's work, has the following sequence: a squire, carrying a lance from which a drop of blood flows, enters the hall. Two squires with candelabra follow him. A maiden comes, bearing a golden Grail ornamented with precious stones and shedding a bright light. Behind the first maiden there is a second one carrying a silver plate. This procession passes on into a second room. A banquet takes place. Two squires bring an ivory table top which is placed upon two ebony stools. During the banquet, the Grail procession files repeatedly through the hall. Perceval fails to ask who is served with the Grail. It is later emphasized that if he had asked about the Grail and the bleeding spear, the wounded Fisher King who ruled in the castle would have been cured.

The German poet's description of this ritual is somewhat different from Chrestien's. Wolfram expands the number of participants in the Grail procession, and the entire ceremony is given a more secular air. And there is another very striking change: Wolfram's substitution of silver knives for Chrestien's silver platter. However, that may have been due simply to the German writer's misinterpretation of the word *tailleor* in his French text; he may have understood it not as "platter" but rather as "cut." The sharp cutting instruments do in any case fit well into the German version's special interpretation of the important question which Parzivâl must ask. If the question which Chrestien's Perceval failed to ask was one of information ("Who is served with the Grail?" "Why does the lance bleed?"), the question that Wolfram's Parzivâl fails to ask is one of compassion, i.e., a question as to the nature of the Grail King's suffering (namely: "Uncle, what is it that troubles you?"). We never learn the function of the lance in Chrestien's unfinished *Perceval;* but in Wolfram's *Parzival* we learn that the lance dripped blood because it was dipped into the Grail King's wound as part of a medical treatment. We discover that the knives were used to scrape from the lance those ice particles which had collected on its tip when it was placed into Anfortas's shivering wound. Through a shroud of "Gothic mystery" we see the significance of the spear and the knives in Wolfram's poem. They are directly connected with Anfortas's suffering, and thus, of course, with the "compassionate" question.

How much of the new interpretation can be attributed to Wolfram himself? Compassionate love, *triuwe,* is a *leitmotif* in both *Parzival* and *Willehalm.* This certainly would account for the reorientation of the question and for the peculiar use of the lance and the knives. Moreover, a major artistic end, both in *Parzival* and *Willehalm* (and this in contrast with the major source of both), is the achievement of a synthesis of the secular and the

spiritual. This might account for the greater richness, the courtly
stylization of the Grail ceremony. Wolfram wished perhaps to
balance out the highly spiritualized aspect of Chrestien's ritual, to
make it more tangible and earthy.[7] Nonetheless, although it
seems rather clear that Wolfram's own sensibilities were somehow
at work reshaping the concept of the Grail, it also seems probable
that the German poet had access to "sources" other than Chrestien. After all, Chrestien himself seems to have known nothing of
the horn of plenty motif and its connection with the Grail. Chrestien does not seem to have been aware of the Grail's power to
impart youthful appearance, and he is seemingly ignorant of the
fact that the Grail could communicate with its keepers, that it had
been held by angels before being entrusted to men, that the Grail
family could count the Knight of the Swan as one of its own.
Other contributors to the Grail legend do, however, have such
information, and Wolfram von Eschenbach shares that knowledge
with them. How might Wolfram have gained access to these, and
possibly other, variants of the Grail story, i.e., to details not provided by Chrestien but available elsewhere?

The twelfth century drew liberally on an inventory of Celtic
narrative stock. Celtic literature, with its journeys into other-
world settings, its magic objects, and its mysterious tests, offered a
body of material quite congenial to audiences hungry for the unusual and to artists seeking to free the imagination. Some believe
that the Grail narratives derive ultimately and essentially from
Celtic lore. Celtic stories involving a king who had a feeding vessel, who lived in an inaccessible realm, as well as Celtic stories
about a king waiting to be cured from a terrible wound, were
probably being told throughout the Middle Ages, and they could
have been transmitted, in more than one form, both to Chrestien
and Wolfram.[8] Others maintain, of course, that the legend of the
Grail should not be traced to Celtic but rather to Christian
"sources."[9] Eighth-century Byzantine liturgy does, for example,
offer some striking parallels to the Grail procession depicted in
Chrestien's *Conte*, and the story of the sacred vessel in Robert de
Boron's *Joseph of Arimathea* (identified as the cup of the Last
Supper) has clearly been shaped by Christian apocryphal writings. But the complicated question of the priority of traditions
and stages of transmission need not concern us here. The evidence
indicates that, by Wolfram's time, both Celtic and Christian mo-

tifs must, in any case, have been gravitating around a holy or mysterious thing, the "Grail," and must have been forming a narrative complex which was, at this critical moment, still in flux, still open to development and capable of striking out in more than one direction. The admittedly vague and difficult situation is further complicated by the possibility of other, more hidden, influences. There are those who believe that the evolving Grail myth was being fed, secondarily, or at the roots, by certain heterodox teachings. Some students of the legend, trying to account for portions of the "esoteric knowledge" attached to the complex, sense, behind the talisman and its cult, doctrines and symbols of Eastern religions or heretical movements.[10]

Wolfram certainly does not help us to resolve the apparent ambiguity. The references he makes to his own sources are highly mysterious and allusive. He speaks of a manuscript written in "magic script" by a certain "vision," Flegetanis, a visionary perhaps, or perhaps a natural scientist, some sort of "scholar," whose background was Jewish on his mother's side and "heathen" on his father's. Flegetanis had divined information on the Grail from the stars, Wolfram says; he had read in the heavens of a sacred object left upon earth by neutral angels. Flegetanis's manuscript, containing this rudimentary information, had been subsequently found in Toledo by Kyot. Kyot was called *laschantiure* (lyric-poet?), and came from the Provence, although he wrote in French. Spurred on by Flegetanis's cryptic references to the mysteries, Kyot had begun to pore through Latin books. He had read chronicles of Britian, France, and Ireland, in order to gain more information. He finally found in "Anjou" the "true tale" of the keepers of the holy object. At another point in his narrative (as if trying scientifically to validate his account), Wolfram also informs us that the *gral,* the stone which produced nourishment for the sacred company, was called *lapsit exillis.*

Wolfram's source citations and the term he applies to the Grail tell us everything and nothing. Scholars have repeatedly tried to explain the Latin designation Wolfram gives to the Grail,[11] and those who take the poet's citations of authority more or less literally have speculated who Kyot (and Flegetanis) could really have been.[12] But none of the theories advanced to explain the stone's name is entirely satisfactory; and no known writers or poets answer to the poet's description of his authorities. Nevertheless,

Wolfram's source citations are, admittedly, tantalizing. They point in so many directions and would "appear" to "explain" the German's plethora of references to the Eastern world, the connection of his Grail story with Anjou, with the Swan Knight and with the variety of motifs from French literature.[13] What better purveyors could there be for all this information than "Flegetanis" and "Kyot"? Jewish culture, "heathen" culture (both of which offer certain analogies to the Grail stone) flowed in Wolfram's time through Toledo and into France by way of the Provence, and the Provence did have its connections with the house of Anjou. Nevertheless, it is difficult to bring oneself to the point of taking Wolfram's appeals to his authorities all that literally, for the source citations do seem part of a game that the German poet was playing with his critics.

Gottfried von Strassburg had insisted that Wolfram's version of *Parzival* could bring *no joy* to noble hearts (*T.* 4676 ff.). Now Wolfram's initial appeal to Kyot seems to be a rebuttal of this accusation, for Wolfram insists, in Book VIII of *Parzival,* that Kyot is an artist whose *particular gift* is making people *happy* (*P.* 416, 21 ff.). Wolfram adds that he is simply rendering Kyot's French into German, the inference being, perhaps, that his work cannot be anything like his rival had charged—to the contrary. If Wolfram's appeal to the Provençal writer has been inserted as some sort of answer to Gottfried's critique, can it then be taken at face value? Gottfried had also complained that Wolfram's manner of speech was very difficult to comprehend; his tale required glossings from the "Black Books," if one was to make any sense of it, he stated (*T.* 4681 ff.). Was not Wolfram simply making humorous use of the material contained in Gottfried's charge, wasn't he merely provoking Gottfried by pointedly telling everyone that the "original source" for his Grail story had "in fact" come from Toledo, that infamous center of necromancy? Wasn't Wolfram mocking his rival's allusions to "Black Books" and to the obscurity of his language by flaunting Flegetanis's "magic" characters, those signs so "difficult" to interpret? Are not many of these points polemical fabrications? Wasn't Wolfram also spinning out his source citations in order to ridicule his rival's scholarly posings? Gottfried had invoked Master Thomas of Brittany as guarantor for the authenticity of *Tristan* and had insisted that he had searched all manner of documents, both Latin and French, in order to be able to offer an impeccable version. Kyot, the guarantor for *Parzival*, had been far more scrupulous than the poet from Strassburg, Wolfram seems to say; *he* had taken cognizance of both "heathen" and Jewish lines of tradition, and had scanned Latin books and the chronicles of *four* lands. Although none of this can, of course, be regarded as conclusive evidence, it does at least argue for the possibility of other than literal interpretations. Kyot and Flegetanis could well be part of an exercise in fabulous source citations (a device not unknown to medieval literature), introduced, in this instance, by a "rural" poet who had been stung by the attacks of an "urban" rival.

In view of this possibility, we must consider whether it is in fact necessary to predicate those manuscripts found in Spain and Anjou, in order to explain Wolfram's stone and the bulk of motifs connected with it. Medieval men were certainly fascinated by the symbolic qualities and alleged powers of precious stones; their lapidaries attest to that. The *lapis elixir*, for example, the philosopher's stone of medieval alchemy, was believed capable of turning base metals into gold; this same stone could also, many believed, serve as an elixir of life. Precious stones were, for these people, something quite mysterious or even holy. Popular imagination did, after all, repeatedly associate these valuable and rare objects with Paradise. The Heavenly City, the Paradise above, was reputedly built of glittering gems; the regions of Earthly Paradise were also supposedly filled with them. Alexander the Great, in the course of his drive far to the East, had, medieval "history" attested, once reached the Garden of Eden. There he had found men in the company of angels. Alexander had procured a precious stone from that blessed place, and this stone was very mysterious and powerful indeed: it changed weight, like Wolfram's Grail; it was, symbolically, like Wolfram's Grail, an admonishment to the proud; and, like Wolfram's Grail, it transmitted something of the power of Paradise; it could give men youth and vitality. Interestingly enough, the Phoenix which, according to Wolfram, derives its power of resurrection from the Grail stone, was actually said to live in or near "Eden." Alexander had seen the bird, which was commonly regarded as a figure and promise of the resurrection, on his journey to the "Garden." [14] Wanderers trying to find the Earthly Paradise would, certain other medieval tales reported, discover the castle of the Neutral Angels along their route, and nearby the realm of Prester John, that fabled Christian king who was, so Wolfram claimed, the son of Feirefîz and Repanse de Schoye, the bearer of the Holy Grail.

There was then somewhere, medieval imagination had it, an Earthly Paradise, like the heavenly one rich in stones and filled with souls impervious to hunger and death. It was hard but not impossible to reach. Does not Wolfram's Munsalvaesche lie within the coordinates of such traditions? The stone of the Grail Castle has a power which is, Wolfram says, very nearly that of "Paradise." Moreover, the stone, which feeds and consoles and wards off death (in analogy to the state of the blessed?), is stored in a "temple"; and the Biblical Temple, as medieval men knew, was a symbol of the kingdom of resurrection, of bliss.

In the multiplicity of motifs surrounding the Grail there is surely some sort of convergence, and behind that convergence, it seems to me, a question. The question Wolfram appears to ask is how the "Paradise State," symbolized by Munsalvaesche revived, may in fact be brought about. Finding the answer to this question would seem to be the ultimate goal of the quest of this poet's hero. Parzivâl's journey to the temple stone, which, like the Paradise stone of Alexander, admonishes the proud, is surely, above all, an inner journey towards himself, towards others, towards God, and ultimately also towards God's kingdom—goals which can only be reached, according to the Bible, through love, purity, and humility, the very virtues which characterize the company at Munsalvaesche and the virtues which the Grail demands of those who would be worthy of it. Parzivâl's struggle seems, then, symbolically a way of realizing the promise of that state of the "blessed," as it was conceived in the myth of Wolfram's own time. It is apparently a journey toward healing, restoration, consolation, and fullness of life, not only for the quester-hero and his uncle Anfortas, but for all mankind, for the Grail Company is a sort of missionary society. The men and women of Munsalvaesche, called by God, go out to guide various principalities of the known medieval world in the West and the East. They come not as Crusaders, under the sign of the Cross, but rather under the sign of illumination and peace, the sign of the Dove and the Paraclete. Is this not Wolfram's answer to the disasters brought about by war with the "heathens," disasters which ensued from the misuse of Papal and Imperial powers? Is not Wolfram's stone a sort of "apocalyptic" figure, a hint of the way to bring about the blessings of God's rule through the agency of men? Are not those called by the Grail in a sense the "living stones" which will, according to Scripture, build "heaven" and bring the reign of peace? [15] These are, admittedly, difficult questions.

The poet's central image, Munsalvaesche, is, in the final analysis an elusive symbol. But that symbol seems fed in any case, by sources the poet could have found in the mainstream of medieval culture; and, whatever the precise constellation of traditions available to Wolfram, it would appear that he himself had much to do with putting them into their final form. [16]

CHAPTER 5

Parzival: *Structure and Meaning*

I *Structure*

A T first glance, *Parzival* seems to be an undisciplined work, an
amorphous tale. Since medieval romances were presented in
installment form, subordinate units had special weight. The poet
was tempted to digress and pursue themes that had generated
applause and interest. Given the serial character of the genre,
these digressions were not unjustified.

In medieval times, the materials required for writing down a
tale were expensive, and even if he could write the poet was
nevertheless forced to keep much of the concept of the work in his
head. Numbers were a relatively simple device for controlling the
various segments of a work and a simple means for seeing that the
proportions were maintained. Numbers do play an important role
in the structure of Wolfram's *Parzival*, controlling proportions of
the romance. Wolfram composed in thirty-line sections, i.e., in
units designed to fit into the length of a normal parchment page;
his Grail poem consists of eight hundred twenty-seven such sections.[1] This story was to be, above all, that of Parzivâl who first
enters the narrative in Book II (*P.* 109, 1 ff.). The earlier portion
(from 108, 30 backwards) is devoted to the adventures of Parzivâl's father Gahmuret, to Gahmuret's winning of two women, the
Mooress Belakâne, and the fair Herzeloyde, Parzivâl's mother.
The pivotal section of Wolfram's tale is Book IX, which describes
Parzivâl's critical meeting with the hermit, Trevrezent. It would
seem that, originally, the tale was to have begun at the point at
which Parzivâl is introduced and was to have consisted of seven
hundred twenty thirty-line segments. At any rate, proceding on
the theory that the original Prologue was to have consisted of one
thirty-line segment, and then counting from 109, 1 ff. to the end of
Parzival (*P.* 827, 30), we do arrive at the number seven hundred
and twenty. Book IX (*P.* 433, 1–502, 30) consists of precisely sev-

enty thirty-line segments. Now the section 827, 1–30 is devoted to the conclusion of the work. If we count from P. 109, 1, to the beginning of Book IX, and from the end of Book IX to 826, 30, we discover that the two longer sections (before and after the pivotal one) consist of precisely three hundred and twenty-four lines each. Given the single thirty-line section as Prologue—we arrive at the following scheme:

$$1 \quad / \; 324 \; / \; 70 \; / \; 324 \; / \; 1 = 720$$

The pivotal Book IX, along with the Prologue and the conclusion, would comprise precisely ten percent of the entire work. Now we must remember: a basic structural feature of Wolfram's tale is that it is a *Doppelroman*. Although primarily the story of Parzivâl, the bulk of the tale is actually almost equally divided between Parzivâl and Gâwân. Here numbers again seem to play a role in controlling the proportions. If we omit Book IX (i.e. P. 433, 1–502, 30), we find that the narration is essentially concerned with Parzivâl from 109, 1, to 337, 30, and with Gâwân from 338, 1, to 432, 30. Again, the narration is concerned essentially with Gâwân from 503, 1, to 731, 30, with Parzivâl from 732, 1, to 826, 30. If we accept this division, we arrive at the following scheme:

$$1 \; \begin{matrix} \text{Parzivâl I} \\ + \, 229 \end{matrix} \; \begin{matrix} \text{Gâwân I} \\ + \, 95 \end{matrix} + 70 \; \begin{matrix} \text{Gâwân II} \\ + \, 229 \end{matrix} \; \begin{matrix} \text{Parzivâl II} \\ + \, 95 \end{matrix} + 1 = 720.$$

However, the balance which the author achieved between these two figures of the *Doppelroman*, is not simply one of quantity.[2] The roles of these two figures are formed in such a way that they illuminate one another. In Book VI, set at the Arthurian court, both Gâwân and Parzivâl are abused, Gâwân by Kingrimursel, and Parzivâl by Kundrîe. In order to restore their honor both set out from the court and take great hardships upon themselves. The culmination of the adventures of both men is to be found in their raising of a spell of sorrow that presses upon two castles. Gâwân frees "Schastel marveile" and becomes its lord while Parzivâl frees Munsalvaesche and becomes its lord. The former rulers of each of the two castles, Clinschor and Anfortas, were stricken in their sexual members, and were both punished for excess of passion. But if there are similarities between Gâwân and Parzivâl and their quests, the two characters also function as contrastive figures. When in Book VI (at the court of Arthur) both Gâwân and Parzivâl are publicly dishonored, Gâwân reacts calmly, wisely, with an unshaken faith in God. Parzivâl, on the other hand, surrenders to rage and blasphemes God. Gâwân and Parzivâl belong, in fact, to different spheres, Gâwân to the Arthurian *sippe,* and Parzivâl to the *sippe* of the Grail. And although Parzivâl falls more deeply than Gâwân, he is also destined to be raised above him. An inner need drives Parzivâl to seek the Grail, whereas Gâwân is bound to seek it only through his given word. Parzivâl finds the Grail, and Gâwân does not. Gâwân's world is that of the courtly gentleman and Parzivâl's that of the lonely seeker with an unusual destiny. Wolfram reinforces these differences in his description of the landscapes through which each of these figures moves.[3] Gâwân's adventures take him through a world of meadows, flowers, gentle plains, exotic trees, the *locus amoenus,* the stylized world of conventional pleasure, the world of human habitation, while Parzivâl's adventures take him through forbidding forests, rugged mountains, trackless wastes, through an uncharted world void of conventional pleasures.

The work exploits, then, the structural possibilities of the *Doppelroman,* and an appreciation of the interplay between the worlds of Gâwân and Parzivâl is essential to an appreciation of the whole. But Wolfram's *Parzival* is not only a *Doppelroman;* it is, at the same time, an Arthurian romance with all the structural implications of this form. In an Arthurian romance, the hero's progress is measured by his distance from Arthur's court, the fixed pole to which the hero comes, whence he departs, and where he returns. Parzivâl's first encounter with the Arthurian court propels him into the quest for knightly honor; the second encounter begins with the confirmation of his knightly honor, but ends with its loss. Parzivâl's third encounter results, of course, in the reconfirmation of his knightly honor. This was a traditional scheme; its models were, above all, Chrestien's *Perceval* and Hartmann's *Iwein.* It is characteristic of the scheme that the Arthurian court should be the scene for moments of external culmination, and for the proclamation of the hero's worthiness or unworthiness to achieve his quest.

With this reference to the Arthurian genre we have not exhausted the structural properties of the work. The Arthurian stations provide an opportunity for external recognition of achievement. But Parzivâl's way is not one that points primarily towards external recognition of achievement. Parzivâl's way moves, above all, through inner growth toward spiritual illumination. There are, then—to counterbalance the stations of external recognition—stations that point the way toward inner growth. They are represented by the instructions of Herzeloyde (Book IV), Gurnemanz (Book V), and Trevrezent (Book IX). These stations are the framework for a span of inner development, reaching from the "state of nature," through the "rule of law" to the "state of grace," reaching from the simple instructions given to a simple boy, through the introduction to the rules of courtly conduct, to the initiation into the meaning of the Grail. And we see Parzivâl acting in a way that corresponds to each. We see first the simple boy, graced with the finest qualities, yet propelled by his drives to desert his mother, and to kill the courtly Ither. Then we see the young knight, his impulsiveness now controlled by the code of courtly conduct, and yet blind to larger meanings and connections. Finally, we see Parzivâl in a state of freedom, at one with himself, with the world of law, and with the will of God. We see the hero in a state characterized by "form" *and* "spontaneity."[4]

These stations are part of the basic structure of the work, and they have an organic quality which permeates the entire artistic plan. Most of the figures moving through the work are somehow affected by this structural idea: there are the figures representing the "state of nature" (the anti-Arthurians), those representing the "rule of law" (the Arthurians), and those representing the "state of grace'" (the members of the order of the Grail). There are, for example, Orilus, Clâmidê, Meljahkanz, Poydiconjunz, and Meljanz, anti-Arthurians, who are characterized by their surrender to passions of the flesh, and anger. There are Gâwân, Arthur, Ginovêr, and the rest—Arthurians, characterized by courtly self-control and grace, but a religiosity that is conventional. Finally, there are the members of the *sippe* of the Grail, i.e., Parzivâl, Sigûne, Trevrezent, and Anfortas, who are characterized by courtliness but also by a religious experience that is deep and genuine. The examples given here are only the obvious ones. The wider implications are to be found throughout the work. Wolfram developed the structural implications of the stations he had found in Chrestien's *Perceval*, but in order to give the structure of the work an even firmer basis, he also tightened the improbable time sequence found in his source. The adventures of Wolfram's Parzivâl take place over a six-year span which is so well calculated that we must conclude that it was significant for the author himself.[5]

The Arthurian court and the Castle of the Grail are ideal worlds, but Wolfram anchors them at both ends, and bends them into the medieval world of political "reality," with the first and last two Books of Parzival. Here, in the adventures of Gahmuret and Feirefîz, contact is established with the world of the East, toward which Western eyes—through the Crusades—were then turned.[6] The Western world had been astonished by the high culture of the "heathen" world, and Christian admiration had grown with time. We see the nobility, the largesse, and the tolerance of the "Bâruc of Baldac," the tenderness and purity of the Mooress Belakâne, whose tears have the sacramental power of Baptism, the prowess and perfect courtliness of Feirefîz. And yet, in spite of all recognition of the cultural achievements of heathendom, Wolfram holds fast to the mission of Christendom. Historical "reality" is clothed in myth: Feirefîz, baptized, and married to Repanse de Schoye—at the conclusion of the poem—is to become the father of the legendary Prester John and, through him, is to bring the religion of Jesus to all of heathendom.

It was a happy stroke on Wolfram's part to anchor the tale's "ideal" world in a more "real" one. And this world of reflected political struggle (which balances the work at both ends) projects itself into the body of the work, i.e., into the world of Arthur and the Grail. Thus the heathen queen Janfûse whiles away the time at Arthur's court and brings word of Feirefîz, of his power and of his quest for his vanished Christian father. Malcrêâtiure and Kundrîe, gifts of the Arab world to Anfortas, appear at crucial points in the work and serve as a reminder of the unbroken thread joining the sphere of East-West confrontation with that of the imagination.

If Wolfram's Parzival has an "ideal" and a "historical" dimension, it also has a "cosmological" one, which (like the first two) is woven into the structure of the whole. The cosmological significance of the tale is expressed in the fateful connection of the world of the Grail with the heavens. Flegetanis had read the story of the Grail in the stars; and the movement of the planets, above all Saturn, brings Anfortas's sufferings to ever recurring climaxes.

When Saturn (the heavenly body which influences temperature) is at its zenith, Anfortas's wound is most agonizing. It freezes so that the spear and the knives are necessary to bring some relief. Saturn's influence is at its greatest during the two supreme moments of the poem, when Parzivâl fails to ask the fateful question and, five years later, when Parzivâl's question brings salvation to the suffering king.[7]

We see, then, that Wolfram's *Parzival* is by no means an undisciplined work. It seems undisciplined, perhaps, because the modern reader fails to detect the hints and make the necessary connections; for it is true that Wolfram is sparing with his clues and reluctant to part with information. He loves to keep his audience in suspense. This is a basic quality of his technique, and, properly understood, it can only contribute to our enjoyment of his poem. We can delight in the manner in which Wolfram shrouds Orilus's and Parzivâl's battle in uncertainty.[8] Do the two recognize each other? Do they understand the real significance of their struggle? In the end, they part understanding, and yet not understanding, each other. Parzivâl has restored Jeschûte's honor, but does he know that Orilus has killed Schîânatulander or that Orilus's brother Lähelîn has usurped his, Parzivâl's lands? We can delight, for example, in the manner in which Wolfram scatters clues as to the identity of the four queens held captive in the "Schastel marveile," until we finally learn that they are, indeed, Gâwân's grandmother, his mother, and his two sisters.[9] Hints, half-concealed clues, and secret links are strewn everywhere (with seeming carelessness) from the hand of the poet. Wolfram plays his role as master of the tale. His technique of heightening suspense is consciously applied and affects the structure of his work. His story reaches its goal, not directly (that would bring less pleasure), but by detours.

II *Meaning*

A *The Prologue*

The Prologue to *Parzival* consists of one hundred and sixteen lines (*P.* 1, 1—*P.* 4, 26); we should note, however, that an additional sixty lines may have been intended as an augmentation to it.[10] These sixty lines—a segment we call the Apologia—are to be found between Books II and III (*P.* 114, 5—116, 4); there is reason to believe that they have been improperly arranged. The

Apologia contains Wolfram's proud proclamation of his name (*P.* 114, 12) and his talents (*P.* 114, 13); it offers a defense of the poet's right to observe and judge feminine character, and concludes with the angry statement that he, the poet, is free of any indebtedness to "books." The verses of the Apologia, if added to the Prologue, would contribute two elements conventionally found in such introductions: the author's name and the reference to a source, a "book." Should we insert the Apologia into the Prologue, there would be no more fitting place to put it than after *P.* 3, 24, at the point at which Wolfram concludes a number of observations and judgments on the female character.

The Prologue was probably not written at a single stroke but rather in two or more stages.[11] There is much to say, for example, for the thesis that verses *P.* 4, 9–26 represent a block older than the other sections.[12] This particular segment is traditional in style and structure and constitutes a self-contained unit. It would have served well as the conventional introduction to a conventional work and may have been the actual Prologue to Wolfram's fragmentary "first edition." The lines *P.* 1, 1–4, 8, on the other hand, with their obscure imagery, their baffling allusions, and their apparently polemic thrust may have been written at a later date, possibly after Wolfram's "first edition" had been criticized, and, perhaps, after the poet had become more convinced of his special talents, and of the particular meaning he wished to implant in his tale.

In the introductory verses of his Prologue, Wolfram does, in any case, attempt to call attention to the nature of the poem's message. To be sure, the initial lines (*P.* 1, 1–14) are obscure and a number of interpretations could be offered. The most convincing one would, however, seem to be the following: the poet begins by arguing that despair and doubt can become bitter to the soul and lead to damnation, but that a dauntless man who doubts and despairs, may, by virtue of his courage, overcome these spiritual barriers and thus be saved. The story of *Parzival* will be the story of a man whose heart is speckled like a magpie: Parzivâl will sin, by "despairing" and doubting God's grace, but he will eventually, by virtue of his tenacity, draw away from such darkness toward the light.[13]

The "foolish" may have difficulty following the "flying" black and white image of the magpie, Wolfram allows; for this category of person the poet's mode of expression will, in fact, twist elusively, like a startled hare (*P.* 1, 15–19). Wolfram further seems to imply that it will be no fault of his if others fail to comprehend his work, and he paraphrases St. Paul to prove the point: a mirror will reproduce the image of a face, but only darkly, Wolfram says (*P.* 1, 20–25). Now St. Paul, in Corinthians, was attempting to call attention to the limitations of language, as a vehicle for the expression of the deepest truths. Wolfram seems to be saying, with Paul as his authority, that his own language may indeed be inadequate to his message, but anyone faulting him will be on weak ground, since, according to Paul, that is simply the nature of things (when one's message is profoundly religious). A person criticizing Wolfram's manner of expression will, therefore, be like a man trying to tear a hair on the palm of the poet's hand, that is, at a point where there are no hairs (*P.* 1, 26–28). After devoting a few more lines to his faithless critics (*P.* 1, 29–2, 4) Wolfram turns his attention to the wise, to those interested in learning from his poem and capable of following its repeated twists and turns (*P.* 2, 5–10).

Were Wolfram's explanation of the message and his defense of the manner of his work, in the initial part of the Prologue, provoked primarily by Gottfried von Strassburg's rejection of the poem? In *Willehalm,* Wolfram refers specifically to critics of his *Parzival,* and Gottfried had indeed condemned the poem's impenetrability, its obscurity, and its barbarous style. Although Gottfried did not mention Wolfram by name, it must have been obvious that it was he who was the object of his scorn (*T.* 4636–4643). Gottfried's conception of the hare jumping about Poetry's heath was a marvelous characterization of Wolfram's truncated syntax and his grotesque verbal formations. Was Wolfram's own reference to the startled hare—in the Prologue to *Parzival*—a well-turned answer to Gottfried's criticism? And was Gottfried one of the dullards incapable of following a flying metaphor? Are, in fact, the Prologue references to false hearts (*P.* 2, 17–22) aimed at Gottfried or his *Tristan*? Are Wolfram's positive references to the pure, modest, and faithful woman, and his condemnation of the beautiful woman with the counterfeit heart (*P.* 2, 23–3, 24) intended as an attack upon Gottfried's Isolde (that beautiful woman who had betrayed her husband with a lover)?

And is the Apologia, too, the product of a feud between these

rivals? In his critique of Wolfram's style, Gottfried had apparently
attacked Wolfram for "perverting" his source. In the Apologia
Wolfram swears that he is independent of the "books" (of
sources?), and that he would rather be surprised naked in his bath
than have his tale considered a "book." With this statement, Wolfram might have sought to reject Gottfried's criticism and, at the
same time, remind his audience of one of the most delicate situations in which Gottfried's Tristan finds himself, the scene in which
Isolde surprises Tristan naked and defenseless in his bath.

Summing up, we must admit that, actually, little is certain in
the ambiguous world of Wolfram's Prologue. The interpretation
offered here is forced to draw much from inference. For Wolfram
poetry is as much an entertainment and a game as it is a vehicle
for profundities. It is quite possible that a desire to play with and
laugh at his critics led Wolfram to push the obscurantism of
which he had been accused to the limits of toleration. Do we hear
him laugh as he unveils—and veils—the deeper meaning of his
tale? In the following translation of the first thirty lines of *Parzival,* I have attempted to capture the provocative mixture of the
two "voices" of the Prologue and of the work, that of the profound
poet and that of the playful "bumpkin":

> If doubt [despair?] is the neighbor of a heart not whole,
> that may [must?] grow bitter for the soul.
> bespattered and bespangled, both,
> is the heart of mottled cloth,
> 5 speckled like a magpie bird:
> when manful and undeterred
> such a man can save his soul,
> for in that man both play a role—
> hell, and heaven too.
> 10 All of hellish hue
> is the inconstant heart,
> blackened in its every part:
> but he of constant wit
> holds to white every bit.
> 15 This flying image I invoke
> is too quick for stupid folk,
> they can't think it through:
> it flees and turns askew
> just like a startled hare.

20 Tin on back of glass will glare
   a form, but—as in the dream
   of blind men—that form will seem
   a most inconstant gleam,
   a dark and gloomy beam:
25 only short-lived joy is there.
   whoever thinks to pluck the hair
   from my palm where none will grow
   knows some tricks that I don't know.

B Gahmuret and Gâwân

The world in which Parzivâl's father lives and dies is, geograph-
ically, broad but spiritually narrow. All the men of Gahmuret's
sphere are knights who struggle to win fame and the love of
courtly women. These relatively simple goals are the boundary of
their wishes.[14]

In his portrayal of the courtly adventures of Parzivâl's father,
Wolfram sometimes takes up an ironic stance. His description of
Gahmuret's entrance into Zazamanc, for example, is a kindly de-
flation of the dandy knight errant whose ego demands much
pomp. It is surely to be taken humorously when Gahmuret, con-
scious of the impression he is making, sends all his entourage before him: ten pack animals, twenty squires, the cooks and serving
boys (who feel self-important), twelve noble youths, battle
horses, drummers, flute players, and fiddlers. More clearly ironic is
the description of Gahmuret's grand entry into Kanvoleis: pages
go before him bearing all those one hundred spears made in Spain
especially for the tourney; the music plays, and Gahmuret's ele-
gantly booted leg, draped over the front of his horse, twitches as
he sights the queen. He rises up to look at her like a hunting
falcon who has found his prey. Gahmuret seems something of a
fop; he is certainly a ladies' man. At Kanvoleis, he plays out a
tragicomedy of courtly love.[15] He is faced with the just demands
of no less than three women: Belakâne, Herzeloyde, and Am-
pflîse, Queen of France. In this episode, the ritual formality of
that Court of Love projects us into a very rarefied atmosphere and
Wolfram's intent is surely, in part, to satirize it.

But, although Wolfram is having some fun with Gahmuret, his
purpose is serious as well. Gahmuret's adventures are just as often

depicted with a sense of awe, and Wolfram's grief at Gahmuret's death is genuine. The epitaph which the poet writes for him is meant sincerely:

> Gahmuret was er genant,
> gewaldec künec übr driu lant.
> ieglîchez im der krône jach:
> dâ giengen rîche vürsten nâch.
> er was von Anschouwe erborn,
> und hât vor Baldac verlorn
> den lîp durch den bâruc.
> sîn prîs gap sô hôhen ruc,
> niemen reichet an sîn zil,
> swâ man noch ritter prüeven wil.
> er ist von muoter ungeborn,
> zuo dem sîn ellen habe gesworn:
> ich mein der schildes ambet hât.
> helfe und manlîchen rât
> gap er mit staete vriunden sîn:
> er leit durch wîp vil schärpfen pîn.
> er truoc den touf und kristen ê:
> sîn tôt tet Sarrazînen wê
> sunder liegen, daz ist wâr.
> sîner zît versunnenlîchiu jâr
> sîn ellen sô nâch prîse warp,
> mit ritterlîchem prîse er starp.
> er hete der valscheit an gesigt.
> nu wünscht im heiles, der hie ligt.   (P. 108, 5–28)*

Here are all the virtues of the conventional Christian knight. Gahmuret is brave, pious and loyal, at least in the accepted feudal

---

* "Gahmuret was his name, a mighty king over three countries. Each one avowed him a crown and rich princes followed after. He was born in Anjou and before Baghdad he gave his life for the Baruch. His fame towered so high that no one shall achieve its equal, however knights may be esteemed. The man is not born of mother to whom his courage vowed surrender—I mean any who works at the knightly trade. Help and manly counsel he unfailingly gave his friends; for women's sake he endured sharp pain; he was baptized and supported the Christian law, yet his death was a grief to Saracens. This is true and no lie. All his years of reason his bravery so strove for fame that he died with knightly glory. Over treachery he triumphed. Wish him bliss who lies here!"

sense. In Parzivâl, Gahmuret's *art* lives on. The most significant factors in this heritage of the heart are manly courage and a passion for love that runs deep in the veins and back to that early ancestor who took a fairy mistress. Wolfram's motif of fairy love is a symbol of disordered emotion, and such emotion is to be a fateful factor in Parzivâl's development.[16]

Gâwân is a typical representative of that same world to which Gahmuret belongs by birth and nature.[17] Gâwân is the Arthurian paragon. Fame and love are also his major concerns. He leaves the court of Arthur and prepares for battle in order to preserve his reputation. He is ready and always at the service of a damsel or a lady in distress. Women mourn his departure; they line the route along which his adventures take him, crowning the battlements and filling the great halls. The typically Arthurian apotheosis of Gâwân's way is that Marvelous Castle, housing no less than four hundred women who wait to be saved by a knight who can successfully survive some preposterous test.

Gâwân is the model of form, courteous and elegant, given to reasonable solutions instead of violent ones. Like Gahmuret's, his Christianity is a relatively comfortable thing and fulfills the requirements of convention. He serves Arthur, but with powers attributed to God. He calls upon divine help for himself and others, hears the mass, and even seeks the Grail, but—and this is what matters—it is a given vow rather than an inner force of soul which causes him to search for it. His inner world, like Gahmuret's, is narrowly bounded, and Wolfram occasionally envelops it in a haze of irony. Commenting on the unusual snowfall at Pentecost (in Book VI), he says:

> Artûs der meienbaere man,
> swaz man ie von dem gesprach,
> zeinen pfinxten daz geschach,
> odr in des meien bluomenzît,
> waz man im süezes luftes gît!
> *diz maere ist hie vast undersniten,*
> es *parriert* sich mit snêwes siten.   (P. 281, 16–22)*

* "Arthur is the man of May, and whatever has been told about him took place at Pentecost or in the flowering time of May. What fragrance, they say, is in the air around him! But *here this tale is cut of double fabric* and *turns* to the color of snow." [Italics mine]

In speaking of the double color of spring and winter, Wolfram uses the same word as in the Prologue, to describe the double color of the magpie: *parriert*. There would seem to be a connection. In his Prologue Wolfram hinted that he was not about to provide a conventional tale of the conventional Arthurian hero, about a hero all white, but rather about one who was speckled. Here in Book VI, Wolfram makes sport of that world of King Arthur, which he apparently judges to be all too free of unpleasant realities. Gâwân's often exaggerated courtesy is ironized in scenes like the one in the Marvelous Castle when Gâwân, after having undergone the most incredible tortures, opens his eyes, and lying in his own blood, says to the damsels attending him:

> "daz ir mich soldet vinden
> sus ungezogenlîche ligen!
> ob daz wirt von iu verswigen,
> daz prüeve ich iu für güete.
> iur zuht iuch dran behüete."   (*P*. 576, 22–26) *

The whole complex of *minne*, so typical of the Arthurian world, is, in part, similarly handled. In the precocious statements which he puts into the mouth of little Obilôt in Gâwân's first adventure (Book VII), Wolfram plays with the content and form of courtly love. He depicts Gâwân's second alliance with tongue in cheek, portrays the battle of the lovers, Gâwân and Antikonîe, in the mock-heroic vein and permeates this narrative with double meaning and good-humored obscenity (Book VIII). The adventures of the love slave Gâwân culminate in the indignities he must suffer at the hands of the imperious Orgelûse. Here (in Books X, XI, XII, XIII that sort of courtly literature, typified by Chrestien's *Lancelot,* is viewed with a jaundiced eye. The climax of Clinschor's Marvelous Castle, with its jeweled and perilous bed, its four hundred women, and finally, the revelation of identities leading to that ultimate and full harvest of marriages should be seen, I think, as humorous hyperbole, as an intentional exaggeration of the happy ending of Arthurian romance. But, as was the case with Gahmuret, the stance which the poet assumes towards Gâwân is

---

* " 'To think you should find me lying in such an unmannerly position! I would take it as a kindness on your part if you would not mention it to anyone. May your good breeding keep you from doing so!' "

not a simple one. His irony is balanced by admiration for the civilizing qualities of courtly culture and courtly love.

C *Parzivâl's Guilt and Redemption*

Parzivâl's search for the Grail is the journey of a man who moves from ignorance to wisdom and redemption. The Parzivâl of the early Books is seen as an ignorant young fool, well-meaning yet inexperienced, who does not fully comprehend the counsel given to him, who pursues his goal with a touching single-mindedness, repeatedly confusing form with substance. Here precisely would seem to be a significant moment in that black-and-white world. Parzivâl sins, yet ignorance and inexperience are seen as mitigating factors. Wolfram depicts a situation in which good will is posited and even emphasized, but in which, nevertheless, guilt is inevitable, and—paradoxically—personal. Man's heart is speckled like magpie plumage. There are no clear lines delineating Wolfram's answer to the ultimate question of guilt and redemption. Boundaries are obscured by the poet, and so the literary critics are perhaps bound to disagree on the solution to what has become a major problem in the scholarly literature.[18]

Is Parzivâl actually guilty of the death of his mother? Can he really be held accountable for the murder of a relative because he has dispatched an unknown knight in a suit of red armor which he coveted for himself? Did the poet consider Parzivâl guilty in his angry renunciation of God? The boy was, after all, convinced of his own innocence. Is Parzivâl's refusal to attend church for five long years, in the poet's view, a bagatelle or a matter of consequence? Did Parzivâl sin in failing to ask the fateful question before the Grail, and if so, was his failure to ask the question a sin against *triuwe*, i.e., compassionate love? We must admit: Parzivâl was certainly following the advice of Gurnemanz when he remained silent, and the punishment—loss of the Grail and of his honor—does seem to be all out of proportion. But what does the text say?

We find that Sigûne accuses her grieving cousin of lack of *triuwe*:

> ir truogt den eiterwolves zan,
> dâ diu galle in der triuwe

an iu bekleip sô niuwe
iuch solt iur wirt erbarmet hân. . . .   (P. 255, 14–17) *

And Cundrîe accuses him of the same failing:

hêr Parzivâl, wan sagt ir mir
unt bescheidt mich einer maere,
dô der trûrge vischaere
saz âne vröude und âne trôst,
war umb irn niht siufzens hât erlôst?
Er truog iu für den jâmers last.
ir vil ungetriwer gast!
sîn nôt iuch solt erbarmet hân.   (P. 315, 26–316, 3) †

At a later point, however, Sigûne tempers her condemnation:
". . . al mîn gerich / sol ûf dich, neve, sîn verkorn . . .' " (P.
441, 18–19).‡ Wolfram too indicates that Cundrîe's words of
damnation were excessive. She was "ein magt gein triwen wol
gelobt. / wan daz ir zuht was vertobt" (P. 312, 3–4).§ The testimony of the text, then, is ambiguous with respect to the question
of the hero's *triuwe*.

But the hero is guilty of something. When he finally comes to
Trevrezent, much chastened from five years of suffering and
search, Parzivâl confesses that he has sinned: ". . . 'hêr, nu gebt
mir rât: / ich bin ein man der sünde hât' " (P. 456, 29–30).|| And a
little later:

. . . 'mirst fröude ein troum:
ich trage der riwe swaeren soum.
hêrre, ich tuon iu mêr noch kunt.
swâ kirchen oder münster stuont,

* "You had the fangs of a venomous wolf, so early did the gall take
root in you and poison your loyalty [*triuwe*]. You should have felt pity
for your host. . . ."
† " 'Sir Parzival, why don't you speak and tell me why, as the sorrow-
ful fisherman sat there, joyless and comfortless, you did not release
him from his sighs? He showed you his burden of grief. Oh, faithless
[*ungetriwer*] guest! You should have taken pity on his distress.' "
‡ " 'All my censure of you, cousin, I shall withdraw.' "
§ ". . . a maiden much praised for her loyalty but whose courtesy was
consumed in rage."
|| " 'Sir, now give me counsel. I am a man who has sinned.' "

> dâ man gotes êre sprach,
> kein ouge mich dâ nie gesach
> sît den selben zîten:
> ichn suochte niht wan strîten.
> *ouch trage ich hazzes vil gein gote:*
> wand er ist mîner sorgen tote.' (*P.* 461, 1–10)*

Trevezent's reaction to Parzivâl's confession is a sigh and a homily on the essence of pride and rage, an exposition of the fall of Lucifer, of the story of Adam and Cain, of the nature of the human race and of original sin: "'. . . diu sippe ist sünden wagen, / sô daz wir sünde müezen tragen'" (*P.* 465, 5–6).† Like Lucifer, Adam, and Cain, Parzivâl is rebellious, and Trevrezent accuses him:

> "ir müest aldâ vor *hôchvart*
> mit senftem willen sîn bewart.
> iuch verleit lîht iwer jugent
> daz ir der kiusche braechet tugent.
> *hôchvart ie seic unde viel.*'" (*P.* 472, 13–17)‡

Not knowing who it is that stands before him, Trevrezent comments on the man who came to Munsalvaesche and failed to ask the question:

> "der selbe was ein tumber man
> *und vuorte ouch sünde mit im dan,*
> *daz er niht zem wirte sprach*
> *umben kumber den er an im sach.*
> ich ensol niemen schelten:
> doch muoz er *sünde* engelten,
> daz er niht frâgte des wirtes scaden." (*P.* 473, 13–19)§

* "'To me joy is a dream, and grief the heavy burden that I bear. Sir, I will tell you more. Wherever church or minster stood, wherever men spoke God's praise, there no eye, since that time, has ever seen me. I looked for nothing but fighting. *And toward God I bear great hatred,* for he stood godfather to my cares.'" [Italics mine].

† "'. . . Adam's race is a wagonload of sin and . . . we must bear that sin.'"

‡ "'. . . a humble will would have to guard you against *pride.* Your youth could all too easily tempt you to violate the virtue of moderation. Pride has always sunk and fallen.'" [Italics mine].

§ "'That was a foolish man *who took sin away with him, since he said*

When Trevrezent learns Parzivâl's identity, he cries:

> . . . "lieber swester sun,
> waz râtes möht ich dir nu tuon?
> *du hâst dîn eigen verch erslagn.*
> *wiltu für got die schulde tragn,*
> *sît daz ir bêde wârt ein bluot,*
> *ob got dâ reht gerihte tuot,*
> *sô giltet im dîn eigen leben.*
>
> . . . .
> Ithêrn von Kaheviez?
> der rehten werdekeit geniez,
> des diu werlt was gereinet,
> het got an im erscheinet.
>
> . . . .
> mîn swester lac ouch nâch dir tôt,
> Herzeloyde dîn muoter."   (*P.* 475, 19–476, 13) *

But Trevrezent is still not aware that Parzivâl, his nephew, is actually the man who failed to ask the question, thus condemning Anfortas to seemingly endless suffering, until, finally, Parzivâl confesses in his extremity. Trevrezent's reaction is significant:

> "*dô dir got fünf sinne lêch,*
> *die hânt ir rât dir vor bespart.*
> *wie was dîn triwe von in bewart*
> *an den selben stunden*
> *bî Anfortases wunden?*
> Doch wil ich râtes niht verzagn;
> dune solt och niht ze sêre klagn.
> du solt in rehten mâzen
> klagen und klagen lâzen."   (*P.* 488, 26–489, 4) †

---

not a word to the king about the distress he could see in him. I make no reproach to anyone, but he will have *sin* to atone for in not inquiring about his host's affliction.' " [Italics mine].

* " 'Dear son of my sister, what counsel can I give you now? *You have slain your own flesh and blood. If you bring your guilt before God, seeing that you were both of one blood, then if God gives a judgment that is just, you will pay for that with your life.* . . . In Ither of Gaheviez God had revealed the fruits of true nobility by which the world was purified. . . . My sister, too, died because of you, your mother, Herzeloyde.' " [Italics mine].

† " '*God gave you five senses, but they denied you their aid. How did*

And later:

> "mit riwe ich dir daz künde,
> *du treist zwuo grôze sünde:*
> Ithêrn du hâst erslagen,
> du solt ouch dîne muoter clagen."   (*P.* 499, 19–22) *

And finally:

> "Dîn oeheim gap dir ouch ein swert,
> *dâ mit du sünden bist gewert,*
> sît daz dîn wol redender munt
> dâ leider niht tet frâge kunt.
> *die sünde lâ bî den andern stên:*"   (*P.* 501, 1–5) †

The text itself indicates that there is ample reason for believing that Parzivâl actually incurs some guilt in almost every instance; in departing from Soltâne, in slaying Ither, in failing to ask the question, and in renouncing God. Driven on by egocentrism, he does not fulfill the fateful demands of fateful situations, and transgresses the first law of Christian brotherhood, the law of compassion and charity. To be sure, his mother's demands are unreasonable, and Parzivâl does not see her fall as he sets out for adventure. He does not actually know that Ither is of his blood. He only knows that Arthur has granted him Ither's armor. And he remains silent before the suffering of his uncle. That the King is his uncle he cannot know. All this does blur, but by no means obliterates, his responsibility. This, at least seems to be the sense of the text.

---

they help you then, at the wound of Anfortas, to preserve your loyalty [*triuwe*]? Yet I will do my best to give you counsel. And you must not grieve too much. You should in right measure grieve and abstain from grief.' "

* " 'I grieve to tell you this: *you bear the burden of two great sins.* Ither you have slain and your mother too you must mourn.' " [Italics mine].

† " 'Your uncle also gave you a sword, but in taking it you burdened yourself with sin, since your lips, which can speak so well, alas did not ask the question then. *But now let this and your other sins be.*' " [Italics mine].

Actually, one does violence to the poem if one attempts to determine the "degree" of guilt in each case. The poet is not offering legalistic explanations, but is proffering a mystery: a man knowing and unknowing, blinded by the primitive ego with which he is born, struggling with the human condition, "a wagonload of sin," yet gifted with treasures of the spirit that render him responsible. Wolfram's poem bears the broad stamp of an Augustinian view of man. Perhaps Parzivâl fails before the Grail because of his earlier sins, because of his role in the death of his mother, and because of his brutal slaying of Ither. Blinded by these sins, he cannot ask the question. Augustine teaches that *ignorantia, caecitas cordis* (blindness of the heart) is a spiritual disorder, a punishment of sin which darkens the capacities of the human senses. In a similar vein Trevrezent explains to Parzivâl that his five senses failed him when he was confronted with the wound of Anfortas; they did not "preserve" his loyalty (*triuwe*). Is this Augustinian spirituality? Such an explanation certainly does justice to the medieval view and appeals to our sense of proportion.

"The race of Adam is a wagonload of sin. We must bear that sin." That is Trevrezent's—and Wolfram's—view. The primeval sin was that of Lucifer. The disorder that is pride has manifested itself from time immemorial in uncontrolled outbreaks of sexual passion and rage. Such is the significance of Cain's sin, and such is the meaning of the symbol of fairy love that plays such an important role in Parzivâl's spiritual heritage. But not only the world of fairy ancestry, not the Arthurian world (the world of Gahmuret and Gâwân) alone is shaken by erotic passion.[19] In the figure of Anfortas, the Grail world, too, suffers the burden of sexual disorder. Anfortas's hideous wound in the groin was inflicted as he undertook a *minne* adventure unacceptable to the Grail. Trevrezent says:

> "mîn hêrre und der bruoder mîn
> kôs im eine friundîn,
> *des in dûht, mit quotem site.*
>
> . . . .
>
> *Amor was sîn krîe.*
> *Der ruoft ist zer dêmuot*
> *iedoch niht volleclîchen guot.*
> eins tages der künec al eine reit
> (daz was gar den sînen leit)

ûz durch âventiure,
durch freude an minnen stiure:
des twanc in der minnen ger.
mit einem gelupten sper
wart er ze tjostieren wunt
sô daz er nimmer mêr gesunt
wart, der süeze oeheim dîn,
durch die heidruose sîn." (*P.* 478, 17–479, 12) *

Symbols of perverted passion abound in the work. The Marvelous Castle is under the sway of an evil sorcerer (Clinschor) who, once a knight, was taken in adultery and castrated. Clinschor's passion now concentrates itself in hate of the virtuous, and he lives to wreck their lives. In the beginning of time, Wolfram tells us, Adam's daughters surrendered to their passions and ate of forbidden roots that perverted their nature. The result was that they conceived and gave birth to monsters. The results of original sin are, then, tangible in the "myth" of Wolfram's romance. In the course of his journey through the world, Parzivâl is shaken and diverted by these same "primeval" passions, pride, rebellion, rage, and uncontrolled sexual drive. His impatience to ride to Arthur's court borders on anger and results indirectly in a death; and his impatience to obtain a suit of armor is characterized by fits of rage, and leads to a murder. There are also the outbursts of vexed passion in the Castle of the Grail (he might have killed the jester taunting him).

All these factors indicate just where the root of Parzivâl's difficulties lies. He is a primitive. When he first comes to Munsalvaesche, he is not yet worthy of the Grail. He must first acquire wisdom and become master of his heart. The young fool is blinded by rage and by sexual passion as well. In Soltâne, the singing of the birds (topologically connected with the rise of love) fills the boy Parzivâl with longings he cannot comprehend

* " 'My lord and brother chose for himself *a lady, of virtue, so he thought* [Orgelûse Gâwân's beloved]. . . . *Amor* [i.e., the love of passion] was his battle cry. *But that cry is not quite appropriate for a spirit of humility.* One day the king rode out alone—and sorely did his people rue it—in search of adventure, rejoicing in Love's assistance. *Love's desire compelled him to it.* With a poisoned spear he was wounded so in the jousting, your sweet uncle, that he never again was healed, pierced through the testicles.' " [Italics mine].

or control. The poet says that it is Gahmuret's nature that stirs in him. And later, a first affection for Lîâze burdens him with a sorrow which again he cannot understand; that, too, is Gahmuret's nature, the poet reiterates. These sexual difficulties culminate in Book VI. Lost in contemplation of the three drops of blood at Plimizoel, Parzivâl is shaken by love, a passion against which Wolfram rails:

> frou minne, ir pflegt untriuwen
> mit alten siten niuwen.
> ir zucket manegem wîbe ir prîs,
> unt rât in sippiu âmîs.
> und daz manec hêrre an sînem man
> von iwerr kraft hât missetân,
> unt der friunt an sîme gesellen
> (iwer site kan sich hellen),
> unt der man an sîme hêrren.
> frou minne, iu solte werren
> daz ir den lîp der gir verwent,
> dar umbe sich diu sêle sent.   (P. 291, 19–30) *

When Parzivâl comes to Arthur's Pentecost at Court he quickly surrenders to that other passion, rage. Disgraced before the Round Table, cursed, and shut out from Munsalvaesche, he renounces God and, from this point on, bears hate for Him in his heart. This is the nadir of Parzivâl's spiritual journey. But Parzivâl shows not only hereditary weakness but hereditary strength of heart as well.[20] There is the manly courage inherited from his father, and the *triuwe* (compassion and compunction) inherited from his mother. Parzivâl possesses *scham* ("modesty," a natural sense of right and wrong) and the *zuht* (courtly propriety) taught by Gurnemanz. And *zuht*, like *scham*, can be an aid in channeling passion. But this is not enough. Wolfram indicates that Parzivâl, although he possesses manly courage, *zuht*, and *scham*, nevertheless fails before the Grail:

* "Lady Love, you are disloyal in ways that are old, yet ever new. You rob many a woman of her good name, you urge upon them lovers blood kindred to them. And it is by your power that many a lord has wronged his vassal, friend has wronged friend, and the vassal has wronged his lord. Your ways can lead to Hell. Lady Love, you should be troubled that you pervert the body to lust, wherefore the soul must suffer."

> waz half in *küenes herzen rât*
> *unt wâriu zuht bî manheit?*
> und dennoch mêr im was bereit
> *scham* ob allen sînen siten.   (*P.* 319, 4–7) *

These virtues are evidently insufficient to make a man worthy of the Grail.

The laws of *zuht* (good breeding) particularly are of limited value, and Parzivâl seems to realize this fact:

> " '*Sol ich durch mîner zuht gebot*
> *hoeren nu der werlte spot,*
> *sô mac sîn râten niht sîn ganz:*
> mir riet der werde Gurnemanz
> daz ich vrävellîche vrâge mite
> und immer gein unvuoge strite.' "   (*P.* 330, 1–6) †

It is necessary to grow towards control of passions and to progress towards purity of heart. *Zuht* (courtesy, the law of good breeding), with its emphasis on outer form, cannot go to the root of Parzivâl's problem and set him free from servitude to his passions. Only *kiusche*, a purity of the heart which is the gift of God's grace, and *diemuot*, humility, can cure the disorder at its roots. And so Parzivâl must move from Gurnemanz, the spokesman of the Arthurian world, the preceptor of true courtesy, to Trevrezent, the pure of heart and spokesman of the world of the Grail. Trevrezent diagnoses the spiritual sickness and charges Parzivâl:

> "diu gotheit kan lûter sîn,
> si glestet durch der vinster want,
> und hât den heleden sprunc gerant,
> der endiuzet noch enklinget,
> sô er vom herzen springet.
> ez ist dechein gedanc sô snel,

* "What help to him now was his *brave heart*, his *manliness and true breeding* [*zuht*]? Still another virtue was his, a *sense of shame.*" [Italics mine].
† " '*If I am to hear the scorn of the world because I obeyed the law of courtesy* [*zuht*], *then his counsel may not have been wholly wise.* It was the noble Gurnemanz who advised me to refrain from impertinent questions and resist all unseemly behavior.' " [Italics mine].

ê er vom herzen für dez vel
küm, ern sî versuochet:
des kiuschen got geruochet." (*P.* 466, 20–28)*

Parzivâl comes to illumination through his sojourn with Trevrezent. God had shown pity and bestowed upon him the gift of His
grace; the horse had borne the young knight straight to the hermit
and the counsel he so sorely needed. At first glance, the development may seem sudden or artificial but that is not the case. After
the catastrophe of Book VI, Parzivâl disappears. We glimpse him
only occasionally until, in Book IX, we see him acquire new insight. This much is true. Parzivâl's level of virtue, the natural
level, was judged insufficient in Book VI; but the natural virtues
do provide the base for his redemption. It would appear that courage, *scham, zuht,* and *triuwe* are conceived of as the human chan-
nels through which God's grace can operate. Again, as with all
crucial elements of the poem, the lines are obscured, but this is
more a virtue than a vice. And we are, after all, given hints. At the
beginning of Book IX, Wolfram emphasizes Parzivâl's *scham* and
zuht, and as Parzivâl's first inner movement toward repentance
occurs, Wolfram says:

> dem riet sîn *manlîchiu zuht*
> kiusch unt erbarmunge:
> sît Herzeloyd diu junge
> in het ûf gerbet *triuwe,*
> sich huop sîns herzen riuwe.
> alrêste er dô gedâhte,
> wer al die werlt volbrâhte,
> an sînen schepfaere. (*P.* 451, 4–11) †

What we seem to have here is an organic progression in which the
way to redemption moves through "natural" to "supernatural"

* " 'Only the Deity can be so pure and bright that it pierces this wall
of darkness, like a rider running to the attack, but soundless and un-
seen. There is no thought so swift, as it springs from the heart, but
that, before it can pass from the heart out through the skin, it is already judged by God. Pure thoughts He approves.' "

† "His manly breeding [*manlîchiu zuht*] inclined him to virtue
[*kiusche*] and compassion. And since the young Herzeloyde had be-
queathed to him true loyalty [*triuwe*], repentance arose in his heart.
Now for the first time he thought of his Creator. . . ." [Italics mine].

virtue. Central to this progression is Parzivâl's courage. Wolfram
sees the world, including that of the spirit, in categories of the
knightly calling. Courage is necessary to face battle against an
enemy on horseback, but it is also necessary to face the battle
within one's heart. Courage is required to cope with incomprehensible passions and incomprehensible judgments of God. Between Books VI and IX a development has taken place in Parzivâl, which was hidden from our eyes, but is now tangible. In Book
IX, Parzivâl is chastened. His grief still moves him to passionate
outbursts, but he seems to have moved some distance towards
mastery of his suffering and, therefore, towards mastery of his
rage against God. This development takes place beyond the world
of the Gâwân Books. Trevrezent encourages its direction:

> "dune solt och niht ze sêre klagn.
> du solt in rehten mâzen
> klagen und klagen lâzen.
> diu menscheit hât wilden art
>
> . . . .
> möht ich dirz wol begrüenen
> unt dîn herze alsô erküenen
> daz du den prîs bejagtes
> unt an got niht verzagtes,
> so gestüende noch dîn linge
> an sô werdeclîchem dinge,
> daz wol ergetzet hieze.
> got selbe dich niht lieze:
> ich bin von gote dîn râtes wer." (*P.* 489, 2–21)*

Parzivâl perseveres, and *zuht* gives way to *kiusche,* to the perfect freedom of humility and purity of heart, a state symbolized
by Parzivâl's ultimate achievement of the Grail. There seem to be
contradictory statements on the nature of this achievement. At
one point Trevrezent tells Parzivâl:

* "'. . . You must not grieve too much. You should in right measure
grieve and abstain from grief. Mankind is by nature wild and strange.
. . . If I could give you back your verdant freshness and make your
heart so bold that you would strive and win renown and not despair of
God, you might succeed in achieving such honor that it would be a
recompense. God himself would not forsake you. I am surety for
that. . . .'"

"ir jeht, ir sent iuch umben grâl:
ir tumber man, daz muoz ich klagn.
jane mac den grâl nieman bejagn,
wan der ze himel ist sô bekant
daz er zem grâle sî benant."   (*P.* 468, 10–14)*

But later on he tells him:

"groezer wunder selten ie geschach,
sît ir ab got erzürnet hât
daz sîn endelôsiu Trinitât
iwers willen werhaft worden ist."   (*P.* 798, 2–5)†

Is the contradiction intentional? Is it the expression of the paradox that lies at the root of the work? Did not Wolfram deliberately juxtapose the omnipotence of God with the freedom of man's will?

* " 'You say you yearn for the Grail. You foolish man, I am grieved to hear that. For no man can ever win the Grail unless he is known in heaven and he be called by name to the Grail.' "
† " 'Greater miracle has seldom come to pass, for you have forced God by defiance to make His infinite Trinity grant your will.' "

CHAPTER 6

The Songs and Titurel

I *Wolfram's* Lieder

THE bulk of Wolfram's lyric poems are *Tagelieder* or "Dawn Songs." This genre, a type developed in southern France, varies a basic and rather simple situation. A knight and his lady have spent the night together. They are awakened by a watchman. The sun is rising, and the knight must steal away lest his forbidden love be discovered. The form of Wolfram's Dawn Songs, like their content, is traditional, the medieval Bar.[1] Wolfram evokes the *Tagelied* situation in five of his poems, and it is believed that he played an important role in bringing the genre to Germany or at least in popularizing it there. In the *Lied* designated by the Lachmann edition as 4, 8 (*Sîne clâwen durch die wolken sint geslagen . . .*) the watchman announces that the claws of the day have struck through the clouds, and that the lover now must leave. The lady pleads with the watchman to let him stay, but the watchman argues that the knight would lose his honor and life if he did not hurry. The lady laments that with every rising of the morning star that knight has been taken from her arms but not her heart. Now she is frightened by the watchman's warning song and by the day gleaming through the glass. Knight and lady press heart to heart and take their leave in ever closer embrace. In 6, 10 (*Von der zinnen wil ich gên . . .*) the watchman comes down from the battlements singing his warning song and proclaiming his loyalty. This song, like 4, 8, ends with a lament and close embrace. In 3, 1 (*Den morgenblic bî wahters sange erkôs ein vroue. . .*), the role of the watchman is noticeably reduced. The lady hears his song at dawn and begins her complaint. Day forces its way through the windows. She tries to lock them—in vain. She presses her friend close, the tears running down her cheeks. The lovers' mouths, breasts, arms, and gleaming legs entwine. In 7, 41 (*Ez ist nu tac . . .*) the watchman plays no part at all. The lovers curse the day and embrace so closely that, as Wolfram remarks, "the power of three suns couldn't shine between them." 5, 34 (*Der helden minne ir clage . . .*) is an *Anti-Tagelied*. Here the poet commands the watchman to be silent; he should no longer sing of that "secret love" which always forced lovers to depart with the rising of the morning star. Wolfram concludes this poem with a praise of married bliss, of legitimate union which does not lead to farewells at dawn.

Attempts at ordering the *Tagelieder* chronologically have not been particularly successful. Whether one takes content as a criterion, for example, the tendency toward reduction of the role of the watchman (and thus, implicitly, a gradual movement toward liberation from the genre)—or whether one takes increasing technical perfection (the gradual mastery of form) as a standard, the results are necessarily conjectural. The five Dawn Songs are, in any case, very much in the Wolfram vein. They exhibit a certain sense of humor, rejoice in healthy sensuality, and have, throughout, an intensely plastic and emotional vision of that tender parting moment. The two remaining songs ascribed to Wolfram, though less powerful, do nevertheless show characteristic traits also. 5, 16 (*Ein wip mac wol erlouben mir . . .*) and 7, 11 (*Ursping bluomen . . .*) parody motifs of Minnesang and contain mischievous attacks on a proud lady. 5, 16 concludes, however, with the poet swearing to be on his best behavior. Wolfram's subdued promise to be good to women rather strongly contrasts with his aggressive stance in the Apologia of *Parzival* and indicates, perhaps, a date of composition somewhat later than that of the Grail romance.[2]

II   Titurel

The verse form of *Titurel* seems to be, like the work itself, a unique invention of the poet. Wolfram writes in four-line stanzas. The first line of the stanza has eight accented syllables, the second ten, the third six, the fourth ten. The first, second, and fourth lines are marked by a caesura after the fourth stress. All lines are terminated by feminine rhymes. It is a form which can be adapted to fit either the drama of dialogue or the contemplation of lyric mood; and it has been constructed with an instinct for the shifting perspectives of this highly original poem.[3]

We possess two "fragments" of this little work (which has only been preserved in four manuscripts) The first "fragment" projects us directly into the narrative. The aged King Titurel reflects upon his spent body. The glory of arms and the beauties of love have faded. He entrusts his crown and the Grail to his son Frimutel, who has five children: Anfortas, Trevrezent, Herzeloyde, Schoysiane, and Repanse de Schoye. Kyot of Katelangen wins and weds one of these children, Schoysiane, but she dies while giving birth. "Thus takes the world its end: all sweetness must at last turn sour" (17, 4). Schoysiane's daughter is christened Sigune and is sent to be raised with Condwîrâmurs. After five years she is entrusted to her aunt Herzeloyde. She grows in beauty and virtue. At the same time, the French Queen Ampflise receives a youngster, Schîanatulander, into her care. He is the grandson of Gurnemanz. Ampflise gives the boy into the service of Gahmuret. Love springs up between the two children, Sigune and Schîanatulander, "so pure all the world couldn't find a trace of its darkness there" (46, 3–4). Both children suffer the pangs of a passion they cannot understand or master. They speak of *minne* and try to plumb its secrets. They know that Schîanatulander must prove his worth with deeds. Gahmuret leaves for the Orient. He seeks out the "Baruc of Baldac," taking Schîanatulander with him. Schîanatulander pales from the passion of his love. His heart is heavy. Sigune too grows pale, tortured by the power within her heart. Herzeloyde notices the love which troubles the child. Sigune tells her aunt how she stands on top of the castle, searching for a sign of Schîanatulander, how her joy has fled and how her body shivers and burns. Gahmuret and Herzeloyde approve this *minne*, and the children's bond is sealed.

The second fragment projects us, at another point, directly into the narrative. A dog crashes through the trees of a forest. Schîanatulander catches it and brings it to Sigune. The dog wears a costly collar that is studded with precious stones. It also has a multicolored leash, yellow, green, red, and brown. The dog's name is "Gardeviaz," that is "Guard the track." Sigune sees upon Gardeviaz's collar the following legend: "man and woman (whoever guards well the track), will receive the world's praise and the soul's salvation too" (144, 3–4). Sigune begins to read the story of Clauditte and Duke Enkunaht which is embroidered on the collar. As she reads, Schîanatulander catches fish in a brook. Suddenly the dog breaks loose, cutting Sigune's hands with the jeweled leash. She cannot finish reading the tale. Schîânatulander chases after the dog but is unable to retrieve the animal. He returns and asks Sigune to give up the chase. She refuses and tells him that he will never have her love if he does not find Gardeviaz. Her curiosity has been aroused.

The figures of the poem are already familiar to us: Sigune, whom Parzivâl had met four times on his journey through the wasteland; Schîânatulander, Sigune's friend, whose body Parzivâl had glimpsed in the sorrowing maiden's arms; he had been felled in a joust by Orilus, the proud and impulsive knight. Parzivâl had last seen the virgin bride, Sigune, dead upon her knees over the casket of her beloved in a hermitage. She had spent her days in constant prayer and penance (seeking forgiveness for having been the cause of this young boy's death, for having sent him capriciously on a quest for the hunting dog and leash?). We know the ultimate fate of Sigune and Schîânatulander from Wolfram's tale of Parzivâl and the Grail, but *Titurel* itself appears to end abruptly—well before the final point. Did Wolfram consider the work complete? Or was the final version to have contained Schîânatulander's joust with Orilus? Was it to have told, in addition, of Sigune's four meetings with Parzivâl?

Actually, it is impossible to fix the intended length of the work, or to fit the preserved fragments into some projected whole. Still partial judgments are possible. Within the first and longer fragment we glimpse, for example, something of an ordering spirit, something of the sense for proportion and symmetry.[4] In scholastic dialogue Sigune and Schîânatulander discuss the love that grips them (Stanzas 57 to 66). The first six stanzas alternate regularly, one for the girl and one for the boy, each being assigned three stanzas. The next four stanzas, forming the center of the dialogue, are differently divided, two for the boy and two for the girl. The concluding six stanzas follow the scheme of the first six. These sixteen stanzas (the dialogue on love) constitute the centerpoint of the first "fragment," and the four stanzas (*T*. 63–66) that form the center of these sixteen, contain the quintessence of the dispute on love: that love's power is of the spirit ("minne ist an gedanken" [66, 2]). This "symmetry" supports the theory that the first so-called *Titurel* "fragment" is actually a complete and self-sufficient unit. Perhaps the poet intended to assemble a series of similar self-contained vignettes, to group them around the cen-

tral theme of *minne*.[5] The result might have been a sort of secu-
larized 'legend' dealing with a 'saint,' of courtly love. It may have
been the story of Sigune's guilt and her redemption.[6]

Titurel is probably a composition of the poet's old age. Wolfram himself seems to speak through the lamentations of the spent
Grail King. The poem is an elegy of leave-taking, both resigned
and full of hope. Titurel's constancy (*staete*), his faithfulness to
the truth within himself (*kiusche*), his compassionate love
(*triuwe*), all these will live on in the heart of the Grail King's
children and his children's children. And love that a woman
brings can plant such virtue in the heart of every man: a belief in
the irrepressible power of *minne* to guide the human being and
build his inner life, to overcome the weight of guilt, the obstacles
of some dark tragedy, is in fact the very positive message of this
sometimes melancholy poem. Love, whose force an eyeless man
would feel, and whose endless meaning all the scribes of the
world could not unfold, which shakes monk and hermit, which
presses the helmeted knight into service, which is everywhere on
earth and in heaven, grips two young children. Their joy disappears as the topical symptoms of an Ovidian love sickness shatter
their immaturity. But in their purity of heart they grasp something of the truth: love is compassionate concern for one another;
it is of the spirit and must be constant. And so the formative elements which must guide and refine this blind and driving passion
that shakes them are at hand. The passage of time, the reality of
life must give their love its final shape. Guided by their own positive instincts, then, and by the advice of experienced mentors,
Gahmuret and Herzeloyde, the two children set out on an adventure of the heart. That—in spite of good beginnings—their love
must lead to death and guilt (towards which the second fragment
points) is part of Wolfram's message. But Sigune, who will be (as
the *Parzival* romance tells us) ultimately sanctified by her *minne*
—that is faithful beyond the grave—rises above the tragedy.

CHAPTER 7

Willehalm

I *Plot*
Book I

IN introducing his narrative, Wolfram recapitulates a number
of things for the benefit of his audience: he reminds them that
Count Heinrich of Narbonne had once sent his seven sons out into
the world, without inheritance, advising them to seek their fortune at the court of Charlemagne. However, the poet intends to
pass over the adventures of six of these sons, he says, in order to
concentrate on one of them, Willehalm. Wolfram indicates that he
considers it unnecessary to relate in detail how Willehalm won the
heathen queen Arabel (she left her husband Tybalt, became a
Christian, took the name Gyburg and married the hero). Wolfram
wishes to come directly to the real subject of his tale, namely the
invasion of Willehalm's realm by a heathen army led by Terramêr,
Gyburg's father. Willehalm opposes that great Saracen host with a
"handful" of men. Trumpets blow; the heathen Halzebier and his
Mohammedans attack; the Christians are able to break up their
formations and Halzebier's army is defeated. It is quickly re-
placed, however, by fresh heathen forces led by Noupatris, a gaily
dressed young knight, who serves Amor, the god of love. Noupatrîs and Viviânz (Willehalm's nephew) charge one another. Noupatrîs is killed immediately and Viviânz is mortally wounded, but
is able to stay in the saddle and continue the fight. Terramêr hears
of the initial losses suffered by his forces and commands the main
army to attack. The overwhelming numerical superiority of the
heathens scatters the Christians. Surrounded by screaming enemies and engulfed by the sound of their drums and trumpets, Willehalm despairs at the loss of his army and prays that he may die.
Halzebier, whose forces have, in the meantime, regrouped, appears on the scene, captures eight Christian princes, and strikes

Vivîanz senseless. Willehalm alone manages to escape. His small
band of followers has been annihilated.

Book II

Willehalm finds his nephew Vivîanz lying unconscious near a
fountain. The young man opens his eyes. His last words express
gratitude for Gyburg's generosity toward him. Vivîanz considers
himself to have been unworthy of her help; he prays that God will
reward her. He hopes that he has never been cowardly. He has
tried to serve Willehalm and repay his kindness to him. Vivîanz
dies, believing that the purity of his life will bring him before
God's throne. A fragrance fills the air as Vivîanz's soul leaves his
body. Willehalm reproaches himself; he feels that he is guilty for
having allowed his inexperienced nephew to fight against mighty
warriors. He watches during the night over the corpse, then
mounts his horse at daybreak. He must return to Gyburg. While
trying to make his way through enemy lines, he comes upon Arofel, the Saracen king, who is Terramêr's brother and Gyburg's
uncle. In the combat which ensues Willehalm wounds his opponent. Arofel begs for mercy and attempts to ransom his life.
Willehalm is pitiless, however. He wants to take revenge for the
loss of his army. Willehalm strikes off the heathen's head, clothes
himself in his armor, and then rides on. He finally reaches the
castle in Orange, bringing his wife, Gyburg, news of the disaster.
Sorrowfully she leads him into the bed chamber, undresses him,
treats his wounds, and then embraces him tenderly. After a short
sleep, Willehalm rises, restored. He consoles his wife, asks her to
decide whether he should go or stay. She advises him to seek the
help of King Lôys and his family. Willehalm takes leave of Gyburg, promising to remain faithful to her and to live only on
bread and water until his return. Disguised once again in Arofel's
richly ornamented armor, Willehalm slips through the heathen
army.

Book III

King Terramêr laments his losses. He considers it a miracle that
a mere handful of Christian knights could have done such damage
to his huge army. He swears that his daughter must die and lays
siege to Orange. Terramêr stands below the castle and threatens
Gyburg, who remains steadfast. In the meantime, Willehalm has

been on the road for several days. He arrives in Orleans, where
he takes a humble lodging for the night. The next morning, he attempts to leave the city, but is stopped by an official of the king,
who demands a toll from him. Willehalm explains that he is a
knight and, as such, not required to pay. The official attempts to
use force. Willehalm beheads him, then fights his way free of a
mob. He unseats and nearly kills a knight, who challenges him to
stop. This knight turns out to be Arnalt, Willehalm's brother.
When Arnalt hears of Gyburg's distress, he offers his help. He tells
Willehalm that the king will be holding court in Laon in three
days, and that many important people will be there, the princes of
the realm, in addition Willehalm's own mother, his father, and
four of his brothers. The hero hurries on, anxious to procure the
necessary aid. He stays overnight at a monastery and reaches
Laon on the next day. His wild and warlike appearance sets the
court in consternation. No one greets him. Willehalm had hoped
that the queen, his sister, would intercede for him, but when she
sees him she orders the doors locked. She has no intention of sac-
rificing an army for the sake of Gyburg, she says. A merchant
takes pity on Willehalm and invites him to stay overnight.
Willehalm accepts this invitation. The next morning he arms himself and swears that he will kill the king because of the mockery
he has had to suffer. The sight of his own family, his mother, his
father, and his brothers, gives him new hope, however. He decides to speak to his sovereign and reminds the king that he,
Willehalm, had helped him to gain his throne. The king replies
that he feels obliged to give him aid. The queen opposes her husband's decision. Willehalm is so enraged at his sister's lack of loyalty that he raises his sword to strike off her head. The queen is
able to escape, however. This horrible situation is ultimately resolved by Alyze, the chaste daughter of the royal couple, who
throws herself at Willehalm's feet and begs her uncle not to dishonor his good name by such conduct. Willehalm is ashamed and
places himself at his niece's disposal.

Book IV

Wolfram explains that Willehalm had been tortured by anxiety
for Gyburg, that he had suffered greatly on account of the death
of his followers. This had led to loss of self-control. When Judith,
the queen and Willehalm's sister, hears of destruction of the

Christian army, she too is beside herself. She falls to her knees before the king and asks for his help. The king is now reluctant to extend his aid (although Willehalm's entire family have promised to help). A meal is served, and the hero bides his time. When the king has taken his fill, Willehalm begins to speak, arguing that not only Orange, but the whole realm has been attacked. Lôys answers that he must take counsel before he can make a decision. Impatient and angry at this hesitation, Willehalm tries to harm the king but is held back by his brothers. The king faces a dilemma: if he acts, he will be giving way to intimidation from a vassal; if he does not act, he will seem to be a coward. He finally decides to help. He proclaims that an army of the realm will gather within ten days. Willehalm remains at Laon. He must recuperate from the wounds of battle. During his enforced sojourn, while watching squires at sport, he observes a huge boy carrying water pails, badly clothed, but with the strength of six men. The squires begin to tease this youth and spill his water. Finally the young giant catches one of his torturers and dashes him to pieces. The king explains that the youth had been brought to him from Persia by merchants and that he was put to menial work because he had refused to become a Christian. Willehalm wishes to take the powerful heathen, Rennewart, into his service, in order to educate him. The young giant requests and receives a huge stave as weapon. After the appointed ten days have passed, King Lôys sets out to meet his army. Rennewart is excited and leaves his stave behind, but he is able to retrieve it. The court stops for the night at the monastery in which Willehalm had lodged some days before. The next morning, they all proceed to Orleans where Lôys entrusts his army to Willehalm. Rennewart takes leave of Alyze, whom he secretly loves. The Christian forces now rush to the aid of Gyburg. As they approach Orange they see a fire.

Book V

During Willehalm's absence, Terramêr tries to intimidate Gyburg. She answers him by praying to the creator of the universe; His might, she says, is the source of harmony in all things; through Christ this God has burst the gates of hell asunder. Terramêr replies that he is unable to believe that Christ, who died so miserably, could possibly be God. The heathen king spends his days alternately threatening and pleading with his daughter. In the course of the siege, Saracen leaders come to Terramêr and request that he command his army to return to sea since there is danger of plague so near the city. Terramêr agrees under the condition that he be allowed to make one more attack. In the course of this attack, the outer city falls and is set afire. Gyburg retreats into the inner city. Frustrated again, Terramêr's forces march towards the coast. The flames of this last attack were the flames Willehalm had seen as he was approaching Orange. The French dash in and discover that the enemy is no longer there. They camp before the city. A festive meal is ordered. Willehalm's father praises Gyburg's steadfastness. Had she not been so loyal, Orange would have been lost. She is an example of the power of love, he says. Gyburg, however, weeps; she feels that she is the cause of death for so many, both heathen and Christian.

Book VI

Gyburg and Willehalm retire for the night to their bed chamber. Their embrace is a source of joy and helps to repay them for all they have suffered. In the meantime Rennewart is restless. The pages torment him. He hopes to find a place to sleep in the kitchen, but the cook burns his beard and face. Rennewart laments this degrading treatment. In a monologue he reveals that he is Terramêr's son. Gyburg comes in the morning to console him. In her heart she feels that he is of her blood. She asks Rennewart to tell her his lineage but he does not betray himself. He is angry and swears that he will revenge himself on his family for failing to free him from his demeaning life. Gyburg outfits Rennewart with a suit of magnificent armor. At a banquet, which takes place on the same day, Gyburg addresses the assembled Christian leaders. She begs them to listen to the plea of a simple woman, that, if victorious, they spare the heathens, who are the creation of God's own hand. She asks the Christians to remember that, whatever the Saracens may have done, God himself forgave those who put him to death. After the meal is ended, Willehalm's army breaks camp and takes the road to the sea. The battle will soon be joined. God alone knows its outcome.

Book VII

Rennewart rushes to see the formations; he is so distracted by all the pomp that he leaves his stave behind for the second time.

Willehalm sends a messenger to retrieve it, but the weapon is so heavy that it has to be transported in a wagon. The Christians camp for the night. On the next morning, Rennewart forgets his stave a third time. In his shame he secretly runs off to fetch it, asking himself whether this may be a test of God to see if he is truly brave. In the meantime, the Christian army has drawn near the heathen camp. When the knights of King Lôys see the tremendous size of the enemy forces, they are overcome by fear and flee. Rennewart, who is returning with his weapon, sees them fleeing through a narrow pass and blocks their way. They are without armor and unable to resist the giant's strength. Rennewart attacks the cowards, inflicting terrible losses, until they finally swear to go back with him and fight under the Christian banner. Terramêr has heard by now of the approach of Willehalm's army. He cries for revenge, lays claim to the throne in Aachen and the authority of Rome. Terramêr sets up the order of battle. Halzebier is to spearhead the attack once again. Eight hundred trumpets blow. The opposing forces strike at one another, like a sword gliding into a sheath.

Book VIII

The Christian vanguard clashes with its Saracen counterpart, led by Halzebier. Rennewart fights violently. He sometimes attacks both men and horses, both heathens and Christians. The pressure of the Mohammedan army increases as their numbers grow. The army of the Christian realm is surrounded, and broken up, but is able to regroup. Rennewart takes revenge for the shame he has suffered by killing many heathens. Then the Saracen king Poydwîz strikes the French in the flanks with a mighty contingent. Up to this point, the battle has raged without advantage for either side. Now the Christians are sorely pressed. They raise their battle cries and resist as best they can. Terramêr attacks with the largest of the heathen armies. Drums and trumpets sound. Troops in exotic armor, with strange devices, pour down upon Willehalm's tiny force. A terrible slaughter ensues, so that the poet is almost unable to continue his narrative.

Book IX

Wilfram intones a prayer to Gyburg, the "saintly" woman; he wishes to see her one day in Paradise. He begs her help for him-

self and for all those who have fought in her behalf. He then
continues his description of the onslaught of Terramêr's army. It
floods over the entire field of battle. The Christians fight back
with bitter intensity. One by one, they are able to strike down the
enemy leaders, the Saracen kings. Halzebier's forces, the first to
have gone into battle, are now exhausted. They fall back to the
sea and their ships. Rennewart pursues them and frees the eight
French noblemen captured by Halzebier in the first battle, two
weeks earlier. These nobles now make a concerted attack on
Halzebier. The heathen warrior has the strength of six but he is
wounded and exhausted. The eight Frenchmen surround and kill
him. Further advantages are gained by Rennewart and Willehalm, although the Saracens continue to throw fresh forces into
the battle. Rennewart swings his stave so mightily that it bursts
apart. He now discovers the sword which has hung so long at his
side. The élan of the heathen has been broken by the death of
Halzebier. The Mohammedans flee and the Christians pursue
them. Rennewart and Willehalm storm on; they come upon Terramêr, fighting a delaying action, surrounded by his sons. Willehalm wounds Terramêr. The heathen youth Kanlîûn tries to protect his father; Rennewart, striking him down, unknowingly kills
his own brother. The resistance of the Saracens is now completely
broken. Terramêr is carried to his ship. A trumpet sounds the
battle's end. Wolfram accuses the Christians of a great sin, the
slaughter of the heathens. All men are a creation of God's own
hand, the poet says. Willehalm surveys the aftermath of the battle: Rennewart has disappeared. Willehalm attributes his victory
to the strength and courage of this young giant. He laments his
loss as a pain greater than that which he suffered at the death of
Viviânz. Brother Bernart admonishes Willehalm and tells him to
collect the captured heathen kings and hold them as a ransom for
Rennewart, who may himself have been captured by the enemy.
Willehalm then speaks with Matribleiz, the noble Saracen, who is
a relative of Gyburg. Willehalm shows compassion. He wishes to
express his reverence for the lineage of Terramêr, which is that of
his wife. He asks Matribleiz to take a contingent of heathen prisoners, to gather up the fallen Saracens, and to carry them away to
their own country, so that they might be buried according to Mohammedan ritual. Matribleiz is moved by this generous offer,

takes the bodies of his comrades, and departs from Willehalm's lands.

II *Sources*

In introducing his second major work, *Willehalm*, Wolfram informs us that it was Hermann of Thuringia who acquainted him with the story. Its French title was *Kuns Gwillâms de Orangis*, he tells us (*Wh.* 3, 11). "Noble Frenchmen have found the tale pleasing," the poet insists, "they have given testimony that there was never an adventure more sweet, true, or solemn; neither additions nor deletion have falsified it" (*Wh.* 5, 8–13). We have no reason to doubt the veracity of Wolfram's claim that Hermann helped him gain access to the French material on which he intended to base his narrative. However, we can hardly accept his claim that the material had been (or would be) presented without "addition" or "deletion." We shall shortly return to this point.

Willehalm (Guillaume, as the French called him) was of course not the kind of hero Parzivâl had been. He was hardly a fairy-tale figure but historical personage of some stature. A grandson of Charles Martel and the Count of Toulouse, he had distinguished himself in defending southern France against Arab invaders, four hundred years before Wolfram's own time. It was said that he had ultimately renounced the world, ending his days as a monk and saint. Poets were attracted by the theme of the warrior-saint's life. In the course of time, they began to circulate *chansons* telling of his deeds. By the thirteenth century, these had blossomed into a large and highly popular cycle of poems with several branches (characterized, as one would expect, more by fervor and fantasy than by fact). One of these branches, the *Bataille d'Aliscans*, told of Guillaume's defense of French soil; it was this work which Hermann had singled out and made available to Wolfram.

The French *Bataille d'Aliscans*, Wolfram's source, starts with the description of a murderous encounter between the heathen army of Desramé and a small Christian force led by Guillaume. The battle is apparently being fought for the possession of Arabella, who is both Desramé's daughter and Guillaume's wife. Arabella has left her father, her heathen husband, and her children. She has become a Christian and has taken the name Guiborc. Guillaume is disastrously defeated in this first engagement. All followers (including his nephew Viviens) are killed, and he must ride to the court of the emperor in order to obtain help. After an unfriendly reception Guillaume is finally given both a new army and the services of a young giant Rainoart. In the second battle against Desramé, Rainoart's incredible strength is decisive. With his help the Christians win a great victory. Rainoart turns out to be Guiborc's brother; he becomes a Christian and marries the daughter of the emperor.[1]

Thirteen relatively complete manuscripts of the *Bataille d'Aliscans* are extant. A comparison of these with one another and with Wolfram's own work indicates that the German poet must have received from his patron a French version of the story in part different from any we know today. This conclusion is at least supported by other evidence. Wolfram, for example, describes two interviews between Terramêr and Gyburg, one directly after Willehalm has left his wife to seek help (109, 17–110, 30), the other shortly before his return (215, 1–222, 9). There is no counterpart to this material in the surviving manuscripts of *Aliscans*. We do, however, find some elements of it in an Old French prose version of the story. This leads us to the conclusion that there must have been a narrative tradition and that Wolfram did not simply invent the important scenes.[2] It is possible that Wolfram had at least passing acquaintance with "branches" of the Guillaume cycle other than the *Bataille*. He is, for example, well aware of the following motifs: he knows that Guillaume's father had disinherited his seven sons and sent them to Charlemagne's court to seek their fortune; he also knows that Guillaume's father adopted a godchild in their stead (cf. *Wh.* 5, 16 ff.); finally, Wolfram refers to a ruse Guillaume once used in capturing the city of Nîmes (*Wh.* 298, 14–16). This sort of information is not to be found in surviving versions of *Aliscans,* but it is in other "branches" of the cycle. There are three possible explanations as to how these and similar allusions may have gotten into the German epic:[3] perhaps Wolfram knew some version of "branches" other than the *Bataille* (e.g. *Nerbonis, Guibers d'Andernas, Charroi de Nîmes*), or perhaps he had received a short (oral) account of such branches from someone else, or possibly the allusions to these "branches" were contained in Hermann's "source," a redaction of *Aliscans* which has since been lost. It must be said that none of Wolfram's references to other branches are so detailed that we must posit actual familiarity with the texts. Wolfram's references do, in fact, show ignorance of certain characteristic features of such texts (as we know them). Of course we must keep in mind, on the other hand, that we do not know all those versions of the various branches which must once have circulated. Furthermore it is unlikely that Hermann would have procured a book containing just a single "branch" of the cycle, namely the *Bataille*. Such poems were, as far as we can tell, usually read in some sort of sequence and therefore bound together. If this assumption is correct, Wolfram could hardly have escaped direct contact with additional material from the cycle. The truth may, therefore, well lie in some combination of all three possibilities mentioned.

It should not surprise us that we are unable to answer all the questions satisfactorily, on the basis of the evidence furnished by documents of the narrative complex. I have attempted to outline at least the major problems, and they do in part result simply from the nature of the genre of the "source." The *chansons de geste* have ancient roots; they are ultimately based on oral traditions, on songs at first memorized and handed down from generation to generation without being committed to parchment; but even after the *chansons* were written down with greater regularity, poets still treated them very much as common property. This popular literary material lived on, in fact, in so many versions that it would be surprising indeed if the "very source" Wolfram used had actually survived. Summing up, we can perhaps say that the narrative matter was well enough known, and it is likely that bits and pieces of the tradition reached the German poet by more than one avenue. These elements could have been stored in his memory and used to supplement any "documents" procured by his patron. Wolfram's introductory reference, denying all "additions" and "deletions," is in any case a common formula. It can not be taken at face value.

We now move the discussion into a related but somewhat different area. In *Willehalm* we find elements for which there is no counterpart in the French tradition, and which could have come from sources to be found in Germany itself.[4] In Book VI, for example, Gyburg makes her plea for tolerance of the heathens. "Hear the advice of a simple woman, spare the creations of God's own hand," she says (*Wh.* 306, 27 f.). In the course of her rather involved argument, she refers to the fact (306, 29 ff.) that the first man God made was a "heathen," as were Elias, Enoch, Noah, and Job. They were all "just," she insists. We do not find this important speech in the French works, but there are passages (similar at least to the segments quoted) in the German *Kaiserchronik* (9418 ff.; 9602 ff.). Furthermore, one of the most striking motifs used in *Willehalm* (not to be found in *Aliscans*; indeed nowhere in the entire Guillaume tradition) is that of the stone *sarcophagi* which miraculously appear to take up the bodies of the Christians fallen in the Battle of Aliscans. The somewhat bizarre detail seems important to Wolfram; he repeatedly refers to it (*Wh.* 259, 4 ff.; 357, 16 ff.; 386, 4 ff.; 394, 20 ff.). We know that Michel de Mouriez, Archbishop of Arles from 1202 to 1217, appealed to all Christendom to support the restoration of one of the churches in the old burial ground of "Aliscans" (Aliscamps). In his appeal, the Archbishop pointed out that this church contained bodies of martyr warriors fallen under the flag of Saint Charlemagne, Saint Guillaume, and Viviens. This plea for help probably would have reached Thuringia, but the letter which documents it lacks the very detail we are searching for. A passage in the *Kaiserchronik* seems again to furnish the answer; it gives an account of *sarcophagi* of supernatural origin quite similar to the one we find in *Willehalm* (14885–908). After a battle against the heathens near Arles, the bodies of fallen Christians were found miraculously resting in beautiful stone coffins, the *Kaiserchronik* says. There is no mention of Willehalm, but the reference to Arles may well have suggested a connection to Wolfram. None of this evidence is conclusive, but it should certainly serve as a warning against binding ourselves to rigid theories postulating some lost French version which provided Wolfram with "everything." The allusions to *Parzival,* to German heroes and myths, to German poets, and to a number of German literary works, for example, could hardly have come from a foreign manuscript.

We are, after all, not hopelessly adrift: the original "source" at Wolfram's disposal was surely not vastly different from the French manuscripts which have survived. Judicious comparisons of the German with the French tradition, based on this assumption, lead to the conclusion that Wolfram's own contribution must have been rather significant. There are too many important "innovations" in *Willehalm* it would be difficult to account for in any other way (it would be really forcing the argument to "insist" that

the bulk of them stemmed from some lost "mediate" source).
These alterations have obviously been introduced as a part of an
"original" and "unified" artistic plan; they demonstrate an intent
to remake not only the style but also the message of this tale.

Let us look, first, at the style. We find in Wolfram's *Willehalm* a
certain penchant for folk wisdom, exemplified by a number of
"homely" sayings which have no parallel in the Aliscans manuscripts. We also find in Wolfram's *Willehalm* a strikingly new
imagery, both bizarre and beautiful, like the imagery of *Parzival*.
We find familiar vocabulary and familiar turns of phrase; the language echoes *Parzival*. All this is not very surprising, of course.
But it is significant that the outer change corresponds to an inner
one, and that both produce an echo. Now the reinterpretation of
the poem's message must have derived from Wolfram, for the
whole cast of the reinterpretation, its preoccupation with the
themes of love, of blood loyalty are completely and undeniably
characteristic of the poet who produced the German Grail romance. One may argue about some of the details but one cannot
deny the general thrust. It would also be unwise to insist upon too
sharp a division when weighing the relative significance of changes
in the language, the content, and the meaning of the work.
Wolfram's style, his vocabulary, and his imagery are hard-won.
He has struggled with them. They are inseparably bound to his
world view.

But let us examine some of the changes. It is instructive to see
what Wolfram has done with the figure of Viviens, for example.[5]
French tradition portrayed Guillaume's nephew as a powerful
warrior and slaughterer of heathens, whose proud heroic code
propelled him into battle. Wolfram's Vivîanz is, on the other
hand, more restrained, almost delicate. The German poet characterizes him as a "sweet" and gleaming *kindelîn,* who is no real
match for strong experienced veterans (67, 28 f.). Wolfram's
Vivîanz is not driven to armed encounters by the hubris of an oath
never to flee an enemy (as was Viviens); his motivation for doing
battle is, above all, loyalty and love. Wolfram seems to see
Vivîanz's death as the pure blood offering of a brave innocent. He
is more a "martyr" than a "hero." It is important to note that the
German poet has introduced young knights very much like
Vivîanz into the ranks of the Saracens. The fragile beauty of these
"heathens" appears doomed by war, just like the "sweetness" of

the Christians; they fight and fall for much the same reason as he: love and loyalty. Now the heathen loyalties are, to be sure, of a very "worldly" nature. Wolfram stylizes his Saracens as perfect cavaliers. Bedecked with jewels, these knights from the Orient serve a cult of courtly love, but precisely because of their services to that cult their hearts are "high" and noble; their sacrifice is "pure"; to those they leave behind their death is as bitter as the death of Viviânz. The Christian Viviânz falls under the standard of the cross, the heathen Noupatrîs under a flag of Amor. But for Wolfram these two signs are not as far apart as we might at first expect. Each in its own way is the symbol of a force at least substantially the same, a force which leads the best warriors in both armies to suffer and to shed their blood. It is the force of love. The German poet is acutely aware of the horrible paradox that love should be so closely entwined with war. He shows how, on both sides, the very "sweetness" of the fallen engenders a fateful bitterness, how the consciousness of a loss deeply felt produces the cry for satisfaction and revenge. Wolfram describes the vicious circle of a war that widens ominously, as one act of violence calls forth another. The despair which the aged poet seems to feel in viewing this drift of human history moves him to reshape the French poem into a great *klage,* a lament, a cry of anguish at the senseless destruction of the beauty of a creation out of God's own hand. For Christians and heathens spring, through Adam, from the same divine father, Wolfram has his Gyburg say. This insistence upon universal brotherhood represents a significant departure from the spirit of the *chansons* whose propaganda tended to represent the enemy as something less than human. The new point of view has undoubtedly been introduced by the same poet who created the "noble heathens" of the *Parzival* romance. But Wolfram can no longer furnish a fairy-tale solution. Universal love seems, in *Willehalm,* something beyond the grasp of humankind. Ignorance and passion are viewed as forces far too powerful. In a world torn asunder by global conflict Wolfram seems to fall back in despair upon the most intimate and tiniest of spheres. The German poet develops the constant love of Willehalm and Gyburg as the central theme of *Willehalm* (again in contrast to his source). He introduces, for example, the two bedroom scenes in Books II and VI. These are important innovations, for they show the power of conjugal love over suffering, as a force which can still the pain of inner wounds, which is a source of strength in darkest hours, and which seems, in fact, to represent the microcosm, the smallest cell, of a solution to the greater problem. For the love of these two appears to have been conceived as a tiny model of the power which could, indeed, cure all the world. Wolfram offers, in *Willehalm,* no Grail Society, no image of a feudal order. He now offers nothing but the moving, changing power of charity, and of a growing loyalty. It is the only thing which could possibly conquer chaos and which might lift the curse of Cain. This power of love emanates, above all, from Gyburg. Here too Wolfram has transformed his source. He has both increased and centralized Guiborc's role. His reinterpretation is based on the poet's simple belief that a woman who is true to her nature can bring grace. Wolfram's Gyburg is bound in affection to both camps, Christian and heathen, and she attempts to "mediate." Her plea for "tolerance" of the heathens in Book VI is perhaps the most significant of all the German poet's innovations; the (blood) loyalties which Wolfram introduces at all levels of his work can only achieve their real significance when they include *all* of God's children. The notions of *sippe, art,* and *triuwe,* so important to an understanding of *Parzival,* are absolutely essential to an understanding of *Willehalm* and the work's plea for universal peace.

III   *Structure and Meaning*

A.   *The Prologue*

There are indications that Wolfram intended his story of Willehalm's role in a murderous war to be taken as a saint's legend.[6] The saint's *vita* was, for example, characteristically introduced with a prayer to the Trinity or with a plea to the Holy Spirit for inspiration. Wolfram's Prologue to his poem is built around *both* these elements of the genre (cf. eg. 1, 1–8; 3, 16–27). Furthermore, Wolfram, in his Prologue, calls explicitly upon the help of *hêrre sanct Willehalm* (*Wh.* 4, 3 ff.), of "Sir Saint Willehalm." He begs the Saint to intercede for him and to free him of the chains of hell. The poet emphasizes the fact that Willehalm once held a shield in his hands, that he once knew the feel of a helmet band and of armor on his body, and that he lived through the pain of battle. Standing now before the throne of God, the Count could not, therefore, fail any knight who cried out for his aid in moments of uncertainty (*Wh*. 3, 12 ff.). These lines appear to explain just how Wolfram wanted his hero to be understood. I would express it in this manner: Willehalm was a man, who, in Wolfram's eyes, had attained holiness while exercising the dangerous calling of knighthood. The poet considered him, therefore, a source of grace for those who had to do the same. One can question such an interpretation, of course. Wolfram does not say with absolute clarity that Willehalm's sanctity was attained through his warrior role. It is possible that the *vita* forms and the title "saint" are brought into play as a sort of reference to the holiness of Willehalm's later secluded monastic years. I do not consider this very likely, however. Wolfram does not speak of Willehalm's monastic life, and everything we know of the poet points to the fact that he considered it his mission to explore the given, to examine reality as the ground upon which man met God. Anyone who could, like Willehalm, emerge forgiving from such a brutal conflict must be some sort of "saint"; that was, I think, the message of Wolfram's work, which he himself called a *süeze rede*, a "holy" tale (*Wh*. 5, 10).

The Prologue does reveal, in any case, Wolfram's understanding of the nature of both God and man. God is pure, Wolfram says, He is the eternal source of power, immensely rich, at work in every fiber of creation, in earth, water, fire, and air, in day and night, and in stones, herbs, and plants. God's depth, His height, and His breadth are unfathomable. God is the father of mankind, *pater noster*. This divine paternity is all important to Wolfram since it brings him, poor and sinful as he feels himself to be, a consolation and a promise that is his salvation from despair. All these themes are Biblical. They represent the faith of both the Testaments, Old and New.[7] They are the hope that the poet manages to wring from the story he is forced to tell.[8]

B.   *The Body of the Work*

As we have indicated, the *Bataille d'Aliscans* was merely a link in a narrative chain. Its beginning assumed a knowledge of Guillaume's abduction of Guiborc and its end set the stage for additional conflicts with the heathens. The *Bataille* was not treated as a closed artistic unit. The French poets strongly emphasized, for example, the deeds of secondary figures, like Vivîanz and Rennewart. These were heroes in their own right, and their actions were central to still other branches of the cycle. The French public,

familiar with the entire narrative tradition, was able to draw upon
its knowledge and to supply the broader framework. Wolfram
was composing for a German audience, however; he could hardly
hope to posit the same familiarity with the larger entity of the
cycle. His position, his narrative point of departure, was, therefore, quite a different one from that of his source. This must have
prompted him to reduce the somewhat expansive thrust of the
French tale, to make his own narrative by contrast relatively self-
sufficient. In Wolfram's version the actions of secondary figures no
longer threaten to exceed the boundaries of the poem; they do not
seek their justification in some wider realm. Wolfram has solved
his major artistic problem in a very simple fashion. He has essentially recast his work around one motif; and that motif was, as we
have seen, conjugal loyalty.[9]

Wolfram has taken still other steps to give his poem a tighter
structure. Willehalm's dash for help and his return are drawn as
mirror images of one another. The hero journeys to Orléans,
spends a night in the city, continues his ride, lodges at a monastery, reaches the court at Laon, spends ten days there, leaves
Laon, lodges at the same monastery as before, meets his army in
Orléans, and proceeds from the city back to the scene of conflict.[10] Particularly the symmetries of time are Wolfram's own contribution. And they appear to have been introduced with a special
purpose. The heathen army attacks the hero's handful of men and
quickly breaks all resistance. After that, little stands between Terramêr and his self-proclaimed goal of revenge. The castle of
Orange may fall at any minute. This would presumably mean
Gyburg's death. Willehalm's hurry, his impatience, his uncontrolled reactions to the indifference of the court—all these stem
from the greatness of his love and his suffering. He thinks constantly of what may be happening to his wife during his absence.
The carefully delineated time structure contributes to our consciousness of the pressure under which Willehalm is forced to act.

All important figures in *Willehalm* must, it seems, learn to function under duress. They try to cope and carry emotional burdens
that are thrust upon them as a consequence of war. Still other
symmetries call attention to this fact. Willehalm's lament for
Viviânz in Book II and his lament for Rennewart in Book IX are
conceived as structural parallels. The same is true of Terramêr's
discussion with Gyburg at the beginning of Books III and V. All

four of these scenes serve as focal points. These moments of narrative pause, of monologue and dialogue help to reveal the inner struggle which must stem from a love forced to exist under the exigencies of conflict. Willehalm is on the verge of despair because of his affection for his young comrades who are dead or lost. Terramêr rages and pleads alternately, so tortured is he by the disaffection of his daughter. Wolfram has, furthermore, taken great care to depict the two battles as events which grow in intensity. The weight given in increasing measure to the end of the work (first battle: 105 thirty-line sections; second battle: 252 thirty-line sections) is indicative of a new cast, that of a rising arc of action which moves toward a horrible culmination.[11] This contrasts with the chain-like linkage of events characterizing *Aliscans* in particular and the heroic genre in general. The structural realignment serves to underscore the fragility of and the danger encompassing human hope.

Wolfram, the aged poet, has projected new structures into the *Willehalm* material, but these obviously do not have the same effect as the structures that were so clearly present in *Parzival*. The structure of the romance pointed to a reliable reassuring order, whereas the structure of the battle epic tends to call attention to the openness and uncertainty of human existence. But Wolfram's *Willehalm* is not a completely pessimistic work. Not only the author's despair, but his hope as well, finds expression in the symmetries of this poem; for the two love scenes, which take place in the bed chamber of the castle, are also conceived as mirror scenes and are certainly to be taken as symbols of something positive. In an act of physical surrender, Gyburg blossoms forth out of "sweet love," like a twisting tendril. With chaste goodness she turns on Willehalm's breast, and her embrace repays him for all his sorrow. Unity of soul and unity of body combine to ward off resignation. In parallel love scenes (the first takes place just after the first battle, the second just before the second battle) Wolfram depicts the restorative power of love. He alludes thereby to the cure of Anfortas, but the possibilities are restricted now. In the battle epic we find no easy lasting cure of ills through the magic ritual of some fairy-tale question put by a predestined hero. The power of love in *Willehalm* is overshadowed; it is not secure and will have to defend itself tomorrow still. When the night of this embrace ends, Willehalm will rise and ride to war. There can be no doubt: the second battle will bring a victory, but it will bring incredible sorrow as well. It will be almost unbearably vicious and destructive.

Parzival and *Willehalm* are based on sources rooted in two very different traditions. It would be dangerous, therefore, to apply our insight into Parzivâl's spiritual way to that of Willehalm—it would, in fact, be doing violence to an example of the heroic genre—in this case *Willehalm*—to expect *significant* religious development in the heart of the central figure. Wolfram does show that he is sensitive to the structual laws of the new form. He gives primary attention to action, i.e., to the struggle between the heathen and Christian worlds. The problem of Willehalm's inner development would seem to be dwarfed by the outer one, by the rush of political events that move inexorably toward the slaughter of the final battle. But precisely because of Wolfram's relentless focus upon the brutal impact of the fighting, the central figure of the epic, Willehalm, is brought face to face with the same spiritual problem as was Parzivâl.[12] The loss of kin in battle and the separation from Gyburg thrust Willehalm into a situation comparable to that of Parzivâl, with his loss of the Grail and his separation from Condwîrâmûrs. Willehalm's initial reaction to suffering is, like Parzivâl's, extreme, i.e., characterized by lack of *kiusche*. Willehalm's violence at the court of Lôys, his brutal treatment of his own sister, and his lack of *zuht* are repeatedly attributed to the suffering that has arisen from the death of so many loved ones and from the uncertainty of Gyburg's position. Willehalm's loss of reason, his erratic surrender to passion are seen, I should think, as being somehow analogous to Parzivâl's early and more primitive state. But if the human condition portrayed in both works is of the same nature, there is certainly a vast difference in degree. Willehalm is shown suspended in a world of sorrow. The outcome is uncertain and his mood is one of *zwîvel;* but Willehalm's *zwîvel* does not provoke an existential crisis, as it did in Parzivâl's case; it does not shatter Willehalm's relationship with God.

That is not to say that Willehalm remains guiltless. Wolfram condemns the hero's excesses. His slaughter of the Persian Arofel is surely viewed as an act contrary to the principles propounded in Gyburg's plea for tolerance. It was an unnecessary and savage deed, this beheading of a helpless foe in the very act of pleading for mercy. Arofel was Gyburg's uncle; he was of her blood, but

Willehalm would not spare the Saracen warrior, although he was
quite aware of the man's relationship to his wife. He was tortured
by the death of Viviânz and demanded the satisfaction of revenge. But contrastive symmetry shows again that the poet
wanted to point to the possibility of reconciliation. At the conclusion of the second battle Willehalm's anguish at the loss of Rennewart is greater than that which he had suffered at the death of
Viviânz in the first. Nonetheless, he is now able to find his way to
new restraint and to forgiveness. Chastened by so much killing, he
now offers a magnanimous proposal to the defeated enemy. He
offers to let a number of them go free, even though this will considerably reduce his bargaining power. Willehalm's motivation is,
significantly, his new-found desire to honor Gyburg's blood, the
blood which flows in the veins of a heathen enemy. This contrasts
with his earlier refusal and failure to exercise temperance and respect for that blood. It is a sign that a certain inner development
has taken place. Willehalm has indeed moved closer to the "sanctity" which the Prologue attibutes to him.

Willehalm is a torso.[13] Wolfram's French source called for the
revelation of Rennewart's identity and for a happy ending of the
young giant's secret love for the emperor's daughter. In his own
poem, the German writer hints at these events, but they fail to
come to pass. The work ends rather abruptly with Matribleiz's
departure from Provence. It is not impossible that Wolfram intended some sort of reconciliation between the opposing forces.
He suppressed, as we have seen, the chanson's harsh portrayal of
the heathens and introduced and repeatedly emphasized the central motif of the Creator-God from whose hands all men spring.
He added, above all, that final tolerant gesture. In the last lines of
the poem, Wolfram's hero recognizes, in a certain sense, the valid-
ity of Mohammedan ritual. He sends the fallen enemies home to
be buried according to their religion. He frees prisoners and, in
surrendering the fruits of victory, moves at last to break the fateful
chain of distrust and revenge.

At the end of this consideration of Wolfram von Eschenbach
(from the perspectives of the past and the present) it is, perhaps,
fitting to ask what the study of his works may hold for the future.
Wolfram's *Parzival* will undoubtedly continue to fascinate
students of literature. It is to be hoped that we will deepen our
understanding of the tremendous variety and the wealth of tradi-

tions flowing into this romance, but that, at the same time, we will further delineate the personal contribution of a very human poet (who so clearly stood both within *and* above his own times). It is to be hoped, above all, that we will turn our attention increasingly toward *Willehalm*. It has become apparent that, in this poem too, Wolfram intended and achieved something quite unique and possibly great. *Willehalm* has been virtually ignored by scholars and critics,[14] but this poem (so expressive of uncertainty and fear, yet so full of courage) may, once properly understood and appreciated, have more to say to modern men than Wolfram's *Parzival*.

Notes and References

Chapter One

1. Cf. Hans Naumann, "Ritterliche Standeskultur um 1200," *Deutsche Vierteljahresschrift, Buchreihe,* XVII (1929). There is controversy about the origin and nature of the "system" of chivalric virtues. A representative selection of articles on this problem has been published by the Wissenschaftliche Buchgesellschaft: *Ritterliches Tugendsystem,* ed. Günter Eifler (Darmstadt, 1970).

2. My depiction of imperial history is based on the standard work of Karl Hampe, *Deutsche Kaisergeschichte in der Zeit de Salier und Staufer* (Heidelberg, 1949), 10th ed.

3. Cf. Joachim Bumke, "Studien zum Ritterbegriff im 12. und 13. Jahrhundert" in *Beihefte zum Euphorion,* I (Heidelberg, 1964).

4. The double interest is reflected in Hartmann's description of the literary matter cultivated at Arthur's court (*Iwein,* ll. 70–73).

5. See the representative selection of articles published by the Wissenschaftliche Buchgesellschaft: *Der deutsche Minnesang,* ed. Hans Fromm (Darmstadt, 1963). An introduction to the various theories on the origin of courtly love may be found in the monograph by Herbert Kolb, "Der Begriff der Minne und das Entstehen der höfischen Lyrik" in *Hermaea, Germanistische Forschungen,* IV (Tübingen, 1958).

6. Cf. Friedrich Heer's provocative chapter "Die Erfindung der höfischen Kultur und die Geburt der europäischen Phantasie" in his book *Mittelalter* (Zürich, 1961).

7. The following is based on Erich Auerbach, "Das abendländische Publikum und seine Sprache" in *Literatursprache und Publikum in der lateinischen Spätantike und im Mittelalter* (Berne, 1958), pp. 177–259.

8. See J. B. Kurz, *Heimat und Geschlecht Wolframs von Eschenbach, Beilage zum 61. Jahresbericht des historischen Vereins für Mittelfranken* (Ansbach, 1916); *Wolfram von Eschenbach. Ein Buch vom grössten Dichter des Mittelalters* (Ansbach, 1930). Wolfram is, according to the author of *der jüngere Titurel,* not from Eschenbach but from *Blienvelden* (1. 579; 1. 5028; 1. 5236). Pleinfeld is located

near Ober-Eschenbach and the Pleinfelder were related with the Eschenbacher.

9. Further geographical references are listed in: Gustav Ehrismann, *Geschichte der deutschen Literatur bis zum Ausgang des Mittelalters,* II[1] (Munich, 1927), pp. 214 ff.

10. The names Wolfram and Wolfelin were common in the family.

11. Reichertshausen gives his information in an *Ehrenbrief.* The *Ehrenbrief* has been printed in the *Zeitschrift für deutsches Altertum* (*ZfdA*), VI (1848), 31–59. The section devoted to Wolfram is found on p. 55. Reichertshausen describes Wolfram's coat of arms: a pot with handle and flowers. Konrad Grünenberg's *Wappenbuch* (end of the fifteenth century) characterizes it in essentially the same way and states that Wolfram was a layman and a Franconian. A second town of Eschenbach (located southeast of Bayreuth) must, with the weight of evidence pointing to Ober-Eschenbach, surrender its claims. Nor does Wolfram's designation of himself as a *Bavarian* (*P.* 121, 7) undermine the position of *Franconian* Ober-Eschenbach. The area in which the Franconian town was located was referred to as *provincia Bajoariorum* and Bavarian law was in force there.

12. As we have seen "knighthood" is no guarantee of nobility. Cf. above p. 15f.

13. In an article by W. E. Gössmann, "Die Bedeutung der Liebe in der Eheauffassung Hugos von St. Viktor und Wolframs von Eschenbach," *MtZ*, V (1954), 205–13, we find the thesis of a connection between the views of marriage held by the German theologian Hugo and the German poet Wolfram. Both Hugo and Wolfram emphasized the sacred quality of the sexual aspect of marriage.

14. Most of the information on Wolfram's patrons has been taken from Albert Schreiber, "Neue Bausteine zu einer Lebensgeschichte Wolframs von Eschenbach," in *Deutsche Forschungen*, VII (1922). Chapters I–V treat: *Wolframs Leser- und Hörerkreis; Wolframs Herr, der Graf Boppo von Wertheim; Wildenberg; Wolfram und Landgraf Hermann von Thüringen; Wolframs Ritterschlag durch den Grafen von Henneberg* respectively.

15. Herbert Kolb, *Munsalvaesche* (Munich, 1963) rejects this generally held view for reasons given on pp. 133 ff.

16. It is, of course, not absolutely certain that the *Wildenberc* (*-burc*) to which Wolfram refers is the one near Amorbach. The actual history of the castle is somewhat obscure. Nevertheless, the arguments amassed by Schreiber are considerable and convincing.

Chapter Two

1. Examples of the influence which learned works may have had (directly or indirectly) on Wolfram are to be found in Ernst Martin's

Commentary on *Parzival* and *Titurel* in *Germanistische Handbibliothek*, IX, 2 (Halle, 1903), xlxii f. The names for the list of Feirefiz's opponents (*P.* 770, 1 ff.) appear in part in the *Polyhistor* of the Roman geographer Solinus, names of stones (*P.* 791, 1 ff.) and of stone experts from ancient times (*P.* 773, 22 ff.) in the *Liber Lapidum* of Marbod of Rennes and the *De virtibus lapidum* of Arnoldus Saxo. Wolfram's knowledge of the heavens would appear to derive from Latin treatises on the subject. Wolfram could have had such information transmitted to him by an "informant" better educated than himself.

2. Wolfram seems to make mistakes in his Latin usage, and his style shows little influence of Latin rhetoric.

3. Cf. *Willehalm*, 237, 3–7.

4. Cf. Blanka Horacek, "Ichne kan deheinen buochstap" in *Festschrift für Dietrich Kralik* (1954), pp. 129–45.

5. Wolfram's confusion of *b* and *p*, *d* and *t*, *g* and *k* could be due to his Bavarian dialect.

6. Edwin Zeydel, "Wolfram von Eschenbach und *diu buoch*," *Euphorion*, XLVIII (1954), 210–15.

7. Carl v. Kraus, "Die *latinischen buochstabe* der 'Klage' V. 2145 ff.," PBB, LVI (1932), 60–74.

8. Two practically applicable stylistic levels were recommended by the medieval books on rhetoric: the *ornatus facilis*, characterized, above all, by figures of repetition (*repetitio, conversio, complexio, adnominatio, traductio*) and the *ornatus difficilis*, characterized essentially by tropes (*metaphora, metonymia, synekdoche, superlatio, katechresis*). *Ornatus facilis* was expected to avoid forced imagery, oddity, excess, artificiality, the very qualities which the *ornatus difficilis* undertook to cultivate. Heinrich von Veldeke, Hartmann von Aue, and Gottfried von Strassburg were certainly adherents of the first style. Some critics believe Wolfram von Eschenbach to have been a practitioner of the second, and certainly there are striking similarities that appear to link Wolfram's use of language with the practices of the dark style, particularly his love for obscure metaphors. Cf. Hennig Brinkmann, *Zu Wesen und Form mittelalterlicher Dichtung* (Halle, 1928); also Leonid Arbusow, *Colores Rhetorici* (Göttingen, 1963).

9. Cf. S. Sawicki, "Gottfried von Strassburg und die Poetik des Mittelalters" in *Germanische Studien*, CXXIV (1932), p. 56 ff; F. Mosselman, *Der Wortschatz Gottfrieds von Strassburg* (The Hague, 1953).

10. Hans Eggers, "*Non cognovi litteraturam* (zu Parzival 115, 27)" in *Festgabe für Ulrich Pretzel* (Berlin, 1963), pp. 162–72. Also Friedrich Ohly, "Wolframs Gebet an den Heiligen Geist im Eingang des *Willehalm*," ZfdA, XCI (1961–62), 1–37.

11. Cf. Ed. Wiessner, "Höfisches Rittertum" in *Deutsche Wortgeschichte*, I (Berlin, 1959).

12. Cf. F. Mosselman, *Der Wortschatz Gottfrieds von Strassburg.*

13. Cf. Ludwig Bock, "Wolframs von Eschenbach Bilder und Wörter für Freude und Leid" in *Quellen und Forschungen*, XXXIII (1879).

14. For a review article on Wolfram's style see Erwin R. Lippka, "Zum Stilproblem in Wolframs *Parzival*: Bericht über den Stand der Forschung," *Journal of English and Germanic Philology* (JEGP), LXII (1963), 597–610. An older but thorough and reliable introduction to the problem is to be found in E. Martin's Commentary to *Parzival* and *Titurel*, pp. lxiv ff. A more recent treatment is to be found in H. J. Bayer, "Untersuchungen zum Sprachstil weltlicher Epen des deutschen Früh- und Hochmittelalters" in *Philologische Studien und Quellen*, X (1962), 199–226. Blanca Horacek argues convincingly for relegation of Wolfram's style to the oral tradition. At the opposite pole we find the theory of Samuel Singer, "Wolframs Stil und der Stoff des Parzival" in *Sitzungsberichte d. kaiserlichen Akademie der Wissenschaften in Wien*, CLXXX (1916), who believes that the dark imagery and the obscure word plays that characterize Wolfram's style must be traced to the *trobar clus* used by Wolfram's Provençal source. The bulk of Singer's argumentation is unconvincing. Ludwig Wolff's article is most helpful; cf. "Vom persönlichen Stil Wolframs in seiner dichterischen Bedeutung" in *Kleinere Schriften* (Berlin, 1967), pp. 262–93.

15. Cf. works listed in footnote 14.

16. Cf. H. Bayer, "Untersuchungen zum Sprachstil weltlicher Epen," p. 207.

17. See Max Wehrli, "Wolframs Humor" in *Festgabe für Theophil Spoerri* (Zurich, 1950), pp. 9–31; also his "Wolfram von Eschenbach Erzählstil und Sinn seines 'Parzival,'" *Deutschunterricht*, VI (1954), 17–40.

18. For an introduction to Middle High German prosody see Siegfried Beyschlag, *Die Metrik der mittelhochdeutschen Blütezeit* (Nuremberg, 1961); also Otto Paul-Ingeborg Glier, *Deutsche Metrik* (Munich, 1964), especially pp. 47–75. E. Martin devotes several pages to Wolfram's prosody in his Commentary, pp. lxxiv ff.

19. Blanca Horacek has written an informative article which points out some of Wolfram's metrical innovations: "Die Kunst des Enjambements bei Wolfram von Eschenbach," *ZfdA*, LXXXV (1954–55), 210–29.

20. See Gustav Hofmann, *Die Einwirkung Veldekes auf die epischen Minnereflexionen Hartmanns von Aue, Wolframs von Eschenbach und Gottfrieds von Strassburg* (Munich, 1930), pp. 1–45. See

also J. F. Poag, "Heinrich von Veldeke's *minne;* Wolfram von Eschenbach's *liebe* and *triuwe*," *JEGP*, LXI (1962), 721–35; "Wolfram von Eschenbach's Metamorphosis of the Ovidian Tradition," *Monatshefte*, LVII (1965), 69–76.

21. A summary of the literature on the Wolfram–Walther relationship may be found in: K. Halbach, *Walther von der Vogelweide* (Stuttgart, 1965), pp. 18 ff.

Chapter Three

1. Cf. Josef Götz, *Die Entwicklung des Wolframbildes von Bodmer bis zum Tode Lachmanns in der germanistischen und schönen Literatur* (Endingen, 1940).

2. Konrad Zwierzina, "Beobachtungen zum Reimgebrauch Hartmanns und Wolframs" in *Festgabe für Richard Heinzel* (1898), pp. 436–511.

3. Elsa-Lina Matz, *Formelhafte Ausdrücke in Wolframs Parzival* (Kiel, 1907).

4. Elisabeth Karg-Gasterstädt, *Zur Entstehungsgeschichte des Parzival* (Halle, 1925).

5. Jean Fourquet, *Wolfram d'Eschenbach et le Conte del Graal* (Paris, 1938), 2. ed. 1966.

6. R. Sprenger, "Die Benutzung des Parzival durch Wirnt von Gravenberg," *Germ.* XX (1875), 432–37.

7. A. T. Hatto, "Zur Entstehung des Eingangs und der Bücher I und II des *Parzival*," *ZfdA*, LXXXIV (1952–53), 232–40.

8. Albert Schreiber, *Neue Bausteine zu einer Lebensgeschichte Wolframs von Eschenbach,* theorizes on the basis of Wolfram's description of helmet ornamentation, the relationship between Christians and heathens, and the references to persons and events of Books I and II, that Books I and II were written after the conclusion of *Willehalm.* The studies of E. Karg-Gasterstädt, *Zur Entstehungsgeschichte des Parzival,* bring her to the conclusion that Books I and II were written directly before or after Wolfram had conceived the plan for Books VI–IX; Julius Schwietering, "Die Bedeutung des Zimiers bei Wolfram" in *Germanica, Festschrift für Eduard Sievers* (1925), pp. 554–82, attempts to prove, by comparing the knightly ornamentation which Wolfram describes at various points, that Books I and II were written after Books III–XVI.

Chapter Four

1. Cf. e.g. M. A. Rachbauer, "Wolfram von Eschenbach. A Study of the Relation of the Content of Books III–V and IX of the *Parzival* to the Crestien Manuscripts" in *The Catholic University of America, Studies in German,* IV (1934); Jean Fourquet, *Wolfram d'Eschen-*

bach et le Conte del Graal (Paris, 1938, 2. ed. 1966); Bodo Mergell, Wolfram von Eschenbach und seine französischen Quellen, II. Teil: Wolframs "Parzival" (Münster, 1943).

2. Friedrich Panzer, "Gahmuret: Quellenstudien zu Wolframs Parzival" in Sitzungsberichte der Heidelberger Akademie der Wissenschaften, philosophisch-historische Kl., I (1939/40).

3. Julius Schwietering, "Einwirkung der Antike auf das Entstehen des frühen deutschen Minnesangs," ZfdA, LXI (1924), 61–82.

4. F. Panzer, "Gahmuret."

5. Wolfram shows that he was familiar with the geography of the Steiermark (cf. P. 496, 15 ff.). It is significant that there was a locality in the Steiermark called Gandîne and that the Steiermark had a panther as its symbol. Moreover, in Wolfram's time the Counts of Steyer were related with the Austrian house of Anschowe. Do we have here an example of Wolfram's attempt to honor a patron by including him in the story, however indirectly? This Austrian background actually represents an argument against Kyot. Albert Schreiber has shown that there may have been reason for Wolfram to be in the Steiermark (see Bausteine, pp. 89–97).

6. Hermann Schneider, "Parzival-Studien" in Sitzungsberichte der Bayrischen Akademie der Wissenschaften, philosophisch-historische Klasse, IV (1944–46); Hildegard Emmel, Formprobleme des Artusromans und der Graldichtung (Berne, 1951).

7. Cf. B. Mergell, W.v.E. und seine französischen Quellen; also W. Richter, "Wolfram von Eschenbach und die blutende Lanze," Euphorion, LIII (1959), 369–79. Richter believes that Wolfram tried himself to reinterpret the lance motif which had not been clearly developed by Chrestien.

8. Cf. e.g. R. Sh. Loomis, "The Irish Origin and the Welsh Development of the Grail Legend" in Wales and the Arthurian Legend (Cardiff, 1956); Jean Marx, "La Légende Arthurienne et le Graal" (Paris, 1952).

9. Cf. e.g. Konrad Burdach, "Der Gral, Forschungen über seinen Ursprung und seinen Zusammenhang mit der Longinuslegende" in Forschungen zur Kirchen- und Geistesgeschichte XIV (1938); Helen Adolf, Viso Pacis. Holy City and the Grail (University Park, 1961).

10. Cf. e.g. Ernst Martin, "Zur Gralsage" in Quellen u. Forschungen, XLII (1880), the Kaaba in Mecca; Paul Hagen, "Der Gral" in Quellen und Forschungen, LXXXV (1900), a meteor stone figuring in oriental cult practices; F. R. Schröder, Die Parzivalfrage (Munich, 1928), Gnosticism; Werner Wolf, "Der Vogel Phönix und der Gral" in Studien zur deutschen Philologie des Mittelalters Friedrich Panzer zum 80. Geburtstag (1950), pp. 73–95, the egg of the bird Ruch;

Herbert Kolb, *Munsalvaesche* (Munich, 1963), the Jewish "stone of exile" connected with the temple cult.

11. *P.* 469, 7: "er heizet lapsit exillis." This reading is from the best ms., D. It is, therefore, probably closest to Wolfram's original intentions. It would seem that the medieval scribes, not understanding what Wolfram meant, attempted to interpret for, we have various forms in the various mss.: *iaspis, lapis, erillis, exillix, exilix, exilis.* Scholars too have attempted to reconstruct the "original" Latin. Some of the attempts are: *lapis ex celis,* "stone from the heavens"; *lapis betillis,* "meteor stone"; *lapis elixir,* "philospher's stone"; *lapis exilis,* "the humble stone"; *lapis ex silice,* the stone of the Easter Fire. The theories are presented and summed up by Joachim Bumke, *Wolfram von Eschenbach* (Stuttgart, 1964), pp. 65 ff., also *Wolfram von Eschenbach-Forschung seit 1945* (Munich, 1970), pp. 250 ff. Acceptance of any one of the theories, including my own [cf. *Monatshefte* LX (1968), 243–244], requires something of an act of faith.

12. Karl Lachmann (1833) accepted Wolfram's statement on Kyot at face value. This view remained essentially unchallenged for some time. Then Karl Simrock, in the third edition of his translation of *Parzival and Titurel* (1857), pointed to the contradictions in Wolfram's description of his source and labeled Kyot a fiction. Wolfram scholarship has since been divided on this question. There are positions of every shading. The boundaries are represented by people like Samuel Singer, "Wolframs Stil und der Stoff des Parzival" in *Sitzungsberichte der kaiserlichen Akademie der Wissenschaften in Wien,* CLXX (1916), and Bodo Mergell, *Wolfram von Eschenbach und seine französischen Quellen.* Singer attributes essentially all of *Parzival* to a French Kyot (Wolfram was then, according to him, little more than a translator). Mergell, in his comparison of Wolfram with Chrestien, on the other hand, is somewhat too eager to attribute the differences found in Wolfram's work to Wolfram himself. A summary of the various positions may be found in the article by Walter Falk, "Wolframs Kyot und die Bedeutung der 'Quelle' im Mittelalter," *Literaturwissenchaftliches Jahrbuch der Görres-Gesellschaft,* IX (1968), 1–63.

13. H. Kolb, *Munsalvaesche* (Munich, 1963) argues in this direction.

14. Cf. F. Ranke, "Zur Symbolik des Grals bei Wolfram von Eschenbach" in *Trivium,* IV (1946), 20–30, reprinted in *Wolfram von Eschenbach,* ed. H. Rupp (Darmstadt, 1966).

15. The figure would have been familiar to Germans. It appears in their vernacular literature. Cf. F. Maurer, *Die religiösen Dichtungen des 11. und 12. Jahrhunderts, I & II.* It is alluded to in *Vom*

Himmelreich, l. 231, *Rheinauer Paulus,* l. 1, *Vom himml. Jerusalem,* l. 1, 3; 7, 1 ff.; 8, 1 ff., *Die Hochzeit,* l. 35, 1 ff., *Rede vom Heiligen Glauben,* l. 182, 8 ff. Cf. also *Kaiserchronik* (ed. H. Massmann), l. 9655 ff.

16. Cf. Bodo Mergell, "Der Gral in Wolframs *Parzival,*" *PBB,* LXXIII (1951), 1–94; LXXIV (1952), 77–159. Although one finds it difficult to agree with the manner in which Mergell has developed the argument, his general thesis—that Wolfram's projection of the Grail is an eclectic one—is not absurd.

Chapter Five

1. Taken from Hans Eggers, "Strukturprobleme mittelalterlicher Epik, dargestellt am *Parzival* Wolframs von Eschenbach," *Euphorion,* XLII (1953), 260–70.

2. Wolfgang Mohr, "Parzival und Gawan," *Euphorion,* LII (1958), 1–22; Marianna Wynn, "Parzival and Gawan. Hero and Counterpart," *PBB, Tübingen,* LXXXIV (1962), 142–72.

3. Marianne Wynn, "Scenery and Chivalrous Journey in Wolfram von Eschenbach's *Parzival,*" *Speculum,* XXXVI (1961), 393–423.

4. W. J. Schröder, *Die Soltane-Erzählung in Wolframs Parzival* (Heidelberg, 1963).

5. H. J. Weigand, "Die Epischen Zeitverhältnisse in den Graldichtungen Chrestiens und Wolframs," *PMLA,* LIII (1938), 917–50.

6. Cf. H. Kuhn, *"Parzival.* Ein Versuch über Mythos, Glaube und Dichtung im Mittelalter" in *Dichtung und Welt im Mittelalter* (Stuttgart, 1959), pp. 151–80, first appeared in *DVjS,* XXX (1956), 161–198.

7. Cf. Wilhelm Deinert, *Ritter und Kosmos im Parzival. Eine Untersuchung der Sternkunde Wolframs von Eschenbach* (Munich, 1960).

8. P. Salmon, "Ignorance and Awareness of Identity in Hartmann and Wolfram: An Element of Dramatic Irony," *PBB, Tübingen,* LXXXII (1960), 95–115.

9. Sidney M. Johnson, "Gawan's Surprise in Wolfram's *Parzival,*" *Germanic Review,* XXXIII (1958), 285–92.

10. Cf. K. K. Klein, "Wolframs Selbstverteidigung," *ZfdA,* LXXXV (1954–55), 150–62; also Hermann Menhardt, "Wolframs Selbstverteidigung und die Einleitung zum *Parzival,*" *ZfdA,* LXXXVI (1955–1956), 237–40.

11. Helen Adolf summarizes the results of older attempts to determine the multistage genesis of the Prologue [*Neophilologus,* XXII (1937), 110–20; 170–85]. H. Rupp has recently argued that the Prologue was written as a single piece [*PBB, Halle, Sonderband* (1961), pp. 29–45].

12. Cf. Hempel, "Der Eingang von Wolframs *Parzival*," *ZfdA*, LXXXIII (1951–52), 162–80. Hempel believes lines 1, 1–4, 8 were written and added to the Prologue after Gottfried's criticism; they are his answer to it. Others are more skeptical about the extent of the interchange between Wolfram and Gottfried. Cf. F. Norman, "The Enmity of Wolfram and Gottfried," *German Life and Letters*, XV (1961–62), 53–97; P. Ganz, "Polemisiert Gottfried gegen Wolfram," *PBB*, (Tübingen) LXXXVIII (1966–67), 68–85.

13. W. J. Schröder, "Der Prolog von Wolframs *Parzival*," *ZfdA*, LXXXIII (1951–52), 130–43, argues that Wolfram's programmatic introduction of a hero who is both "black" and "white" is deliberate, a protest against Hartmann von Aue's overly idealistic portrayals. The critics are not, I should point out, in agreement on the precise meaning of *zwivel* in 1. 1, 1 (is it merely "doubt" or is it "despair of God's grace," the unforgivable sin against the Holy Spirit). Cf. H. Adolf, "The Theological and Feudal Background of Wolfram's *zwivel*," *JEGP*, XLIX (1950), 285–303; also H. Hempel, "Der *zwivel* bei Wolfram und anderweit" in *Erbe der Vergangenheit, Festgabe für Karl Helm* (1951), pp. 157–97. It should also be noted that the word *muoz* in line 1, 1 of the Prologue can be translated in more than one way, either as "can" or "must." I have chosen the first translation and the interpretation which seems to follow from it. A more recent summary of literature on the Prologue may be found in the review article of Henry Kratz, *JEGP*, LXV (1966), 75–98.

14. As I have pointed out, much of this material is taken from my dissertation.

15. Cf. Hermann Weigand, "Three Chapters on Courtly Love in Arthurian France and Germany" in *University of North Carolina Studies in Germanic Languages and Literatures*, XVII (1956).

16. Cf. Hermann Schultheiss, "Die Bedeutung der Familie im Denken Wolframs von Eschenbach" in *Sprache und Kultur der germanischen und romanischen Völker*, B, XXVI (1937).

17. See Georg Keferstein, "Die Gawanhandlung in Wolframs *Parzival*," *Germanisch Romanische Monatshefte*, XXV (1937), 256–74; Wolfgang Mohr, "Parzival und Gawan," *Euphorion* LII (1958), 1–22; Marianne Wynn, "Parzival and Gawan—Hero and Counterpart," *PBB Tübingen*, LXXXIV (1962), 142–72.

18. A summary of secondary literature on the problem of Parzivâl's guilt is contained in Peter Wapnewski, *Wolframs Parzival* (Heidelberg, 1955). Wapnewski himself has shown in detail that Augustinian doctrine is the key to understanding Parzivâl's guilt. For typical earlier literature on the question see Wolfgang Mohr, "Parzivals Ritterliche Schuld," *Wirkendes Wort*, II (1951–52), 148–160 (emphasizes that Parzivâl's sins are against his own blood); Friedrich Mau-

rer, "Parzivals Sünden," *DVjS*, XXIV (1950), 304–46 (this article marks the inception of the Augustinian theory), Julius Schwietering, "Parzivals Schuld," *ZfdA*, LXXXI (1944–46), 44–68 (traces Parzivâl's guilt to his lack of *triuwe*, compassion).

19. The following have written on the central problem of *minne:* Kurt Boestfleisch, "Studien zum Minnegedanken bei Wolfram von Eschenbach" in *Königsberger deutsche Forschungen*, VIII (1930); G. Keferstein, "Zur Liebesauffassung in Wolframs *Parzival*" in *Festschrift für Albert Leitzmann, Jenaer Germanistische Forschungen* (1937), pp. 15–32. Cf. M. Schumacher, *Die Auffassung der Ehe in den Dichtungen Wolframs von Eschenbach* (Heidelberg, 1967), for a thorough treatment of Wolfram's views on marriage.

20. Gottfried Weber emphasizes the role of reason in Parzivâl's growth to maturity: *Der Gottesbegriff des Parzival* (Frankfurt, 1935); see the same author, *Parzival. Ringen und Vollendung* (Oberwesel, 1948); W. J. Schröder points to Parzivâl's growth through *scham* and *zuht* to *kiusche: Der Ritter zwischen Welt und Gott* (Weimar, 1952). Both authors have extremely helpful things to say about the nature of Parzivâl's redemption but their one-sided orientation toward favorite themes of *Geistesgeschichte* has exposed them to criticism. Theories about Wolfram's particular relationship to the intellectual spirit of his time have ranged widely. Wolfram has been portrayed not only as an Augustinian but also as a Thomist (preemptorily), as a Catharist heretic, and even as a forerunner of the Reformation. Wapnewski's book on *Parzival* (the Augustinian theory) and the book by Benedikt Mockenhaupt, *Die Frömmigkeit im "Parzival" Wolframs von Eschenbach* (Bonn, 1942) convincingly demonstrate that the more unusual theories are unnecessary to explain the religious phenomena in Wolfram's work. A survey of the enormous literature on this subject may be found in Hans-Joachim Koppitz, *Wolframs Religiosität* (Bonn, 1958), and, of course, in Bumke's two books on Wolfram.

Chapter Six

1. The Bar form was a three-part form. The first and second parts were identical, and the third part different from the first two.

2. For representative articles on the *Lieder* see the Selected Bibliography at the end of this volume.

3. For a discussion of the form cf. Ludwig Wolff, "Wolframs Schionatulander and Sigune" in *Studien zur deutschen Philologie des Mittelalters, Friedrich Panzer zum 80. Geburtstag* (1950), pp. 116–30.

4. The following is taken from Werner Simon, "Zu Wolframs *Titurel*" in *Festgabe für Ulrich Pretzel* (1963), pp. 185–90.

5. An idea of M. F. Richey, "The *Titurel* of Wolfram von Eschen-

bach: Structure and Character," *Modern Language Review,* LVI (1961), 180–93.

6. See Bernhard Rahn, "Wolframs Sigunendichtung. Eine Interpretation der *Titurel*fragmente" in *Geist und Werk der Zeiten,* IV (1958).

Chapter Seven

1. I have used the summary of Susan Bacon, who worked with the various manuscripts of the *Bataille*. Cf. Bacon, *The Source of Wolfram's Willehalm* (Tübingen, 1910), p. 2.

2. For a summary of the material in the Prose Romance see Bacon, pp. 100 ff.

3. The three possibilities are discussed in some detail by Bacon.

4. Cf. Samuel Singer, *Wolframs Willehalm* (Berne, 1918), pp. 43 f.

5. My treatment of the changes combines ideas of Bodo Mergell and Joachim Bumke, without accepting all the interpretations of either. Cf. B. Mergell, *Wolfram von Eschenbach und seine französischen Quellen, I. Teil: Wolframs Willehalm;* Joachim Bumke, *Wolframs Willehalm* (Heidelberg, 1959).

6. Cf. F. Ohly, "Wolframs Gebet an den Heiligen Geist im Eingang des *Willehalm,*" *ZfdA,* XCI (1961–62), 1–37.

7. Cf. Ingrid Ochs, "Wolframs *Willehalm*—Eingang im Lichte der frühmittelhochdeutschen geistlichen Dichtung," *Medium Aevum,* XIV (1968).

8. W. Schröder, *Minne und ander klage* (Zu *Willehalm* 4, 26), *ZfdA,* XCIII (1964), 300–13, offers an interesting reading of the line in question: Wolfram is informing his audience that his tale is to be one about "love and other suffering." His poem is, indeed, to be a lament.

9. The analysis of the structure of *Willehalm* represents an adaptation of the ideas of J. Bumke, *Willehalm* (Heidelberg, 1959). R. Kienast, "Zur Tektonik von Wolframs *Willehalm,*" in *Studien zur deutschen Phil. des Mittelalters, Friedrich Panzer dargebracht* (1950), 96–115, attempts to show that the work has certain mathematical proportions.

10. Cf. Bumke, *Willehalm.*

11. Cf. Bumke, *Willehalm.*

12. Cf. Werner Schröder, "Zur Entwicklung des Helden in Wolframs *Willehalm*" in *Festschrift für Ludwig Wolff* (1962), pp. 265–76. Bumke has criticized Schröder's interpretation. A controversy has also developed between Bumke and Schröder on the interpretation of certain key concepts in the work. My article on *Willehalm* (cf. Selected Bibliography) attempts to mediate.

13. Ludwig Wolff, "Der *Willehalm,*" *DVjS,* XII (1934), 504–39. There are scholars who consider the work complete. The various argu-

ments are summed up in Joachim Bumke's book on *Willehalm*. Bumke himself argues for a compromise solution, namely that Wolfram started his work intending to solve the wide range of the problems he had introduced, but, in the end, gave up this intention, and fitted the work with a jerry-built conclusion.

14. It is to be hoped that the discussion generated by Bumke's book on *Willehalm* and the establishment of a *Willehalm* Forschungsstelle under Werner Schröder mean that this period of relative neglect is finally at an end.

Selected Bibliography

PRIMARY SOURCES

A. Middle High German Editions

Wolfram von Eschenbach, ed. Albert Leitzmann, 5 Vols., "Altdeutsche Textbibliothek," Vols. 12–16 (Halle and Tübingen, 1948 ff.).

Wolfram von Eschenbach, ed. Karl Lachmann, sixth ed. (Berlin-Leipzig, 1926), A photomechanical reprint is available.

Wolfram von Eschenbach, ed. Eduard Hartl, seventh ed., Vol. I: *Lieder, Parzival* and *Titurel* (Berlin, 1952).

B. English Translations

"The *Parzival* of Wolfram von Eschenbach. Translated into English Verse with Introduction, Notes, and Connecting Summaries," by Edwin Zeydel in Collaboration with Bayard Q. Morgan, *University of North Carolina Studies in the Germanic Languages and Literatures,* V (Chapel Hill, 1951).

Wolfram von Eschenbach *Parzival. A Romance of the Middle Ages.* A New Translation, with an Introduction, by Helen M. Mustard and Charles E. Passage (New York, 1961).

Schionatulander and Sigune. An Episode from the Story of Parzival and the Graal as Related by Wolfram von Eschenbach. Translated with Explanatory Framework, by Margaret F. Richey (Edinburgh-London, 1960). There is at present no English translation of *Willehalm.*

SECONDARY SOURCES

A. Bibliography

PRETZEL, ULRICH-BACHOFER, WOLFGANG. *Bibliographie zu Wolfram von Eschenbach* (Berlin, 1968), second ed. Has 1,062 entries. Selection reaches from earliest period of Wolfram scholarship up to the present. Lists reviews.

B. General Treatment

BUMKE, JOACHIM. *Wolfram von Eschenbach* (Stuttgart, 1970), third ed. A lucid and balanced discussion.

C. Review of Research

BUMKE, JOACHIM. *Die Wolfram von Eschenbach-Forschung seit 1945: Bericht und Bibliographie* (Munich, 1970). An exhaustive review of the secondary literature for the period since 1945. A complete bibliography for this time span is appended and includes reviews as well as unpublished dissertations.

D. Wolfram's Style

*WEHRLI, MAX. "Wolframs Humor" in *Überlieferung und Gestaltung: Festgabe für Theophil Spoerri* (Zürich, 1950), pp. 9–31; "Wolfram von Eschenbach. Erzählstil und Sinn seines *Parzival*," *Deutschunterricht* VI (1954), 17–40. Two thought-provoking essays.

WOLFF, LUDWIG. "Vom persönlichen Stil Wolframs in seiner dichterischen Bedeutung. Ein Versuch" in Ludwig Wolff, *Kleinere Schriften zur altdeutschen Philologie* (Berlin, 1967), pp. 262–93. Examines the elements in Wolfram's style; sees them as a projection of his personality.

E. Parzival

DEINERT, WILHELM. *Ritter und Kosmos im Parzival. Eine Untersuchung der Sternkunde Wolframs von Eschenbach* (Munich, 1960). A careful study of the possible sources for Wolfram's knowledge of the stars. Throws light upon the character and extent of the poet's education.

*EGGERS, HANS. "Strukturprobleme mittelalterlicher Epik, dargestellt am *Parzival* Wolframs von Eschenbach," *Euphorion*, XLVII (1953), 260–70. An attempt to demonstrate that a framework of mathematical symmetries guided Wolfram in his composition of *Parzival*.

KOLB, HERBERT. *Munsalvaesche. Studien zum Kyotproblem* (Munich, 1963). A heavily documented source study which offers arguments in favor of accepting Wolfram's statements on Kyot.

KUHN, HUGO. "Parzival. Ein Versuch über Mythos, Glaube und Ditchtung im Mittelalter," *DVjS*, XXX (1956), 161–98. Reprinted in Hugo Kuhn, *Dichtung und Welt im Mittelalter* (Stuttgart, 1959), pp. 151–80. An effort at analyzing the complex configuration of tradition and the layers of symbolism in Wolfram's *Parzival*.

MERGELL, BODO. "Wolfram von Eschenbach und seine französischen Quellen. II. Teil: Wolframs *Parzival*" in *Forschungen zur deutschen Sprache und Dichtung*, XI (Münster, 1943). Approaches the source problem with the goal of working out Wolfram's artistic intent and personal contribution.

———. "Der Gral in Wolframs *Parzival*: Entstehung und Ausbildung der Gralssage im Hochmittelalter," *PBB,* LXXIII (1951), 1–94; LXXIV (1952), 77–159. An assertion of eclectic symbolic intent in Wolfram's conception of the Grailstone.

MOCKENHAUPT, BENEDIKT. "Die Frömmigkeit im *Parzival* Wolframs von Eschenbach" in *Grenzfragen zwischen Theologie und Philosophie,* XX (Bonn, 1942), reprinted by Wissenschaftliche Buchgesellschaft (Darmstadt, 1968). Illuminates the medieval background of Wolfram's religiosity.

PANZER, FRIEDRICH. "Gahmuret: Quellenstudien zu Wolframs *Parzival*" in *Sitzungsberichte der Heidelberger Akademie der Wissenschaften, Philosophisch-historische Klasse, I* (Heidelberg, 1940). Another study which indicates that Wolfram's "sources" are probably diverse.

*RANKE, FRIEDRICH. "Zur Symbolik des Grals bei Wolfram von Eschenbach," *Trivium,* IV (1946), 20–30. Proposes that the Grail is modeled upon the *lapis exilis,* the "humble stone" of the Alexander legend.

SACKER, HUGH. *An Introduction to Wolfram's "Parzival"* (Cambridge, 1963). Offers a running commentary on the text.

SPRINGER, OTTO. "Wolfram's *Parzival*" in *Arthurian Literature in the Middle Ages,* ed. Roger Loomis (Oxford and New York, 1959), 218–50. A judicious consideration of the major questions in *Parzival* scholarship.

WAPNEWSKI, PETER. *Wolframs "Parzival." Studien zur Religiosität und Form* (Heidelberg, 1955). Examines the Biblical and Augustinian basis for Wolfram's religious views.

*WESSELS, PAULUS B. "Wolfram zwischen Dogma und Legende," *PBB, Tübingen,* LXXVII (1955), 112–35. Theorizes that Eucharistic legends were the source for many of the motifs forming Wolfram's conception of the Grail.

F. Lieder

*MOHR, WOLFGANG. "Wolfram von Eschenbach, *Ursprinc bluomen* . . ." in *Die deutsche Lyrik. Form und Geschichte,* Vol. I, ed. Benno von Wiese (Düsseldorf, 1956), 78–89. Attempts to demonstrate how, in this poem, Wolfram uses shopworn motifs to create something original.

*THOMAS, HELMUT. "Wolframs Tageliedzyklus," *ZfdA,* LXXXVII (1956–57), 45–58. An examination of the metrical form of Wolfram's *Lieder.*

G. Titurel

*WOLFF, LUDWIG. "Wolframs Schionatulander und Sigune" in *Studien zur deutschen Philologie des Mittelalters, Friedrich Panzer zum*

134 WOLFRAM VON ESCHENBACH

80. *Geburtstag* (Heidelberg, 1950), pp. 116–30. A careful discussion of the various problems posed by this work.

H. Willehalm

BUMKE, JOACHIM. *Wolframs "Willehalm." Studien zur Epenstruktur und zum Heiligskeitsbegriff der ausgehenden Blütezeit* (Heidelberg, 1959). Treats sources, structure, and meaning of *Willehalm.*

*KIENAST, RICHARD. "Zur Tektonik von Wolframs *Willehalm*" in *Studien zur deutschen Philologie des Mittelalters. Friedrich Panzer zum 80. Geburtstag* (Heidelberg, 1950), pp. 96–115. An attempt to find mathematical proportions in the structure of *Willehalm.*

MERGELL, BODO. "Wolfram von Eschenbach und seine französischen Quellen. I. Teil: Wolframs *Willehalm*" in *Forschungen zur deutschen Sprache und Dichtung*, VI (Münster, 1936). Also approaches the source problem with the goal of working out Wolfram's artistic intent and personal contribution.

OCHS, INGRID. "Wolframs *Willehalm*-Eingang im Lichte der frühmittelhochdeutschen geistlichen Dichtung" in *Medium Aevum*, XIV (Munich, 1958). A study of the vernacular religious literature in Germany, in so far as it contributes to an understanding of the *Willehalm* Prologue.

*OHLY, FRIEDRICH. "Wolframs Gebet an den Heiligen Geist im Eingang des *Willehalm*," *ZfdA*, XCI (1961–62), 1–37. Treats Wolfram's Prologue, its relationship to the legend, and Latin traditions of the Middle Ages.

POAG, JAMES. "Wortstrukturen in Wolframs *Willehalm*," *DVjS*, XLVI (1972), 82–112. Offers an interpretation of key concepts and passages.

*Those works marked by an asterisk have been reprinted in *Wolfram von Eschenbach*, ed. Heinz Rupp (Darmstadt, 1966).

Index

(The works of Wolfram von Eschenbach are listed under his first name)